100 Days
of
Healing
Daily Devotional

STEPHEN ARTERBURN

HENDRICKSON PUBLISHERS   ROSE PUBLISHING

100 DAYS OF HEALING

Aspire Press is an imprint of
Rose Publishing, LLC
140 Summit Street
P. O. Box 3473
Peabody, Massachusetts 01961-3473
www.hendricksonrose.com

Written with Dena Dyer.

Book cover and page design by Sergio Urquiza.

ISBN: 9781628624946

Printed by RR Donnelley
Guangdong,China
November 2019, 2nd Printing

This book is given to

Debbie

on this day

February 2000

Happy Birthday!

Enjoy this book and
continue living well!

Love your sister & Brother
in Christ,
Debe & Oscar

Contents

Introduction

You and I long for healing in different ways and at different times in our lives. We may seek healing for relationships, finances, physical ailments, spiritual struggles, or emotional abuse. We may long for healing in our marriages, friendships, or thought lives.

We also have many (often unspoken) questions about healing: Why does God not heal me (or my loved one)? Is the miracle of healing worth praying for? How long will healing take? What must I do—if anything—to be healed?

In the one hundred devotions that comprise this volume, we'll explore numerous facets of healing. We'll look at Scriptures, stories, and quotes about healing. Each devotion has a prayer you can pray as you journey toward healing in your own life.

Take time each day to read the additional Scriptures included with each devotion. Seek God with your whole heart—and you will be amazed at the changes he will bring.

DAY 1

The Source of Healing

*He was pierced for our transgressions, he was crushed
for our iniquities; the punishment that brought us
peace was on him, and by his wounds we are healed.*

ISAIAH 53:5

Because we live in an imperfect, sinful world, all of us will experience brokenness. In fact, none of us get through childhood unscathed. And whether our wounds stem from our own disobedience to God or from mistreatment by others or something else entirely, we will often be tempted to become disillusioned or hardened.

However, God desires that we keep our hearts and minds focused on him and that we seek his purposes for our pain and allow him to heal the broken places. Healing is a process that takes time, courage, and self-discipline. When we are persistent about holding our wounds up to the light of Christ, we will eventually discover a level of freedom and contentment we once thought impossible.

Jesus—through his own selfless ministry and his sacrifice on the cross—is the source of true, lasting healing. His love saves our souls and imparts abundant life. We no longer need to be afraid of getting hurt, because his supernatural grace and peace flow through us. We can forgive and be forgiven, living and serving as beloved children of the living God. Ask God where your heart has been hurt and take a step toward healing as you release your broken places to the Lord.

Come, and see the victories of the cross.... Christ's wounds are thy healing … His death thy life, His sufferings thy salvation.

MATTHEW HENRY

If we really believe not only that God exists but also that God is actively present in our lives—healing, teaching, and guiding—we need to set aside a time and space to give God our undivided attention.

HENRI NOUWEN

To be alive is to be broken; to be broken is to stand in need of grace.

BRENNAN MANNING

FOR FURTHER REFLECTION

Matthew 4:23–24; Luke 4:40; Acts 4:10; 9:34

Today's Prayer

Heavenly Father, thank you for your healing power. Remind me to turn to you when I am wounded, and give me courage to submit my broken places to your nail-scarred hands. Amen.

The Healing Power of Jesus

Nevertheless, I will bring health and healing to it;
I will heal my people and will let them enjoy
abundant peace and security.

JEREMIAH 33:6

During the three years of Jesus' earthly ministry, he taught people how to love God and the rest of humanity. He gave us a stunning example of unconditional love when he surrendered to death at his enemies' hands. And everywhere he went, he healed people. He made the blind see, the deaf hear, the lame walk—and he healed diseases of every kind (Matthew 8:16; 11:5).

Naturally, those of us who have illnesses (both visible and invisible) and who believe in his supernatural power pray for physical healing. For some, Jesus answers those prayers with a resounding yes. He heals others in different ways: spiritually, emotionally, relationally, or mentally.

Whatever type of healing you need, go to Jesus. Ask him for mercy, strength, grace, and endurance. If he immediately answers your prayer the way you expect, praise him for his miraculous power. If he doesn't, thank him anyway, surrendering yourself to his plans and timing. The relationship that results from honestly and fervently connecting with Jesus will sustain you.

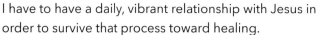

I have to have a daily, vibrant relationship with Jesus in order to survive that process toward healing.

Beth Moore

With love that knew no fear, the Singer caught his torment, wrapped it all in song and gave it back to him as peace.

Calvin Miller

We do not need the sheltering wings when things go smoothly. We are closest to God in the darkness, stumbling along blindly.

Madeleine L'Engle

For Further Reflection

Psalm 145:9; Matthew 12:15;
Luke 7:21-22; Acts 10:38

Today's Prayer

Lord, heal me of everything that needs your tender touch. Help me to trust you as I wait for the ultimate healing in heaven. I praise you for your power and mercy, offered so freely. Amen.

God's Unending Compassion

*Because of the LORD's great love we are not
consumed, for his compassions never fail. They are
new every morning; great is your faithfulness.*

LAMENTATIONS 3:22–23

The world seems to be getting darker by the day. We hear news of school shootings, terrorist attacks, and natural disasters so often that we don't even process all of it, and we often become numb to any more bad news. Psychologists have created a term for this phenomenon: *compassion fatigue.*

Aren't you thankful that God never has compassion fatigue? Indeed, his great love is the reason we do not have to fear the forces of evil. We can look disease, depression, and despair in the eye and say, "You will not win!" Because of our Father's extraordinary love for us and his faithfulness to provide all his precious children need, we will not only be able to survive everything life throws our way, but we will also be able to spend eternity with him in heaven.

Whether the darkness you are facing today comes from a scary diagnosis, relational brokenness, or spiritual warfare, resolve to rest in God's provision. Though your health, friends, or family members may abandon you, your Father never will. Ask him for comfort, and open the Word as often as you can, soaking in the promises he has made.

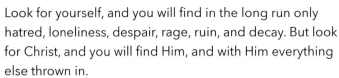

Look for yourself, and you will find in the long run only hatred, loneliness, despair, rage, ruin, and decay. But look for Christ, and you will find Him, and with Him everything else thrown in.

C. S. Lewis

This hard place in which you perhaps find yourself, so painful and bewildering, is the very place in which God is giving you opportunity to look only to Him, to travail in prayer, and to learn long-suffering, gentleness, meekness—in short, to learn the depths of love that Christ Himself has poured out on all of us.

Elisabeth Elliot

God is awesome in power and there is never a time when He is not beside you. He is faithful and holy.

Charles Stanley

For Further Reflection

Exodus 34:6; Psalm 103:13;
Isaiah 49:13; 54:10

Today's Prayer

Gracious God, thank you for the unending compassion you daily pour out on my worn, weary soul. When I am hurting, I need you to comfort me. I am so grateful that you never tire of hearing about or providing for my needs. Help me to extend that kind of compassion to others. Amen.

Seek God to Find Peace

*The peace of God, which transcends all
understanding, will guard your hearts
and your minds in Christ Jesus.*

PHILIPPIANS 4:7

B ecause you're in need of healing, do you feel as if you've lost your sense of peace? Are you currently in the kind of circumstance that makes you question whether you'll ever experience peace again?

When life throws its worst at us, it's hard not to feel as if God has abandoned us. Where we once felt peace, we now feel only despair and doubt. These difficult times test us to the core of our being, and they often feel unending.

Thankfully, our Creator doesn't reject us when our desperate feelings override our faith. In fact, Jesus, who chose to descend from heaven and become a man, experienced things like we do—some things even worse than most of us go through. And just like us, Jesus once cried out, "My God, my God, why have you forsaken me?" (Matthew 27:46; Mark 15:34).

If Jesus (and many other biblical heroes) questioned God, so can we. Be honest with him, because he already knows you are struggling. Then look to the miracle of the resurrection for a fresh infusion of hope. Ask God to renew your mind and allow you to reframe your circumstances in the light of his love. Because of our Savior, our future rests secure.

The only time I ever find my dealings with God less than clear-cut is when I'm not being honest with Him. The fuzziness is always on my side, not His.

CATHERINE MARSHALL

The Old Testament proves that God honors questioners. Remember, grumpy Job emerges as the hero of that book, not his theologically defensive friends.

PHILIP YANCEY

A wound that goes unacknowledged and unwept is a wound that cannot heal.

JOHN ELDREDGE

FOR FURTHER REFLECTION

Psalm 46:8–9; Luke 24:36;
Colossians 3:15; 2 Thessalonians 3:16

Today's Prayer

Merciful Jesus, I admit that my faith often falters. In my humanness, I see only what's in front of me and forget your love is constant and your presence is sure. Give me the peace that is beyond anything I can even imagine. Amen.

DAY 5

Peace Is a Person

Peace I leave with you; my peace I give you. I do not give to you as the world gives. Do not let your hearts be troubled and do not be afraid.

JOHN 14:27

Whether we are seeking physical, emotional, mental, or spiritual wellness (or all four), healing is a journey. It usually doesn't happen overnight, so early on in that journey, we can be filled with anxiety about how and when healing will occur.

We can, however, take comfort in the Scripture for today, for these are the words Jesus said during his very last conversation with his disciples before he was crucified. Please note that Jesus' peace doesn't come with limits—it's not just available to us sometimes or in some circumstances.

So here's the big question: What if we really believed him? What if we trusted Christ—took him at his word—in every situation and difficulty? How would that change our daily lives and impact our decisions?

Today, allow Jesus' courage and strength to infuse your own set of challenges. Notice the difference it makes . . . and then do it again tomorrow.

When life doesn't make sense, we can still have peace.

RICK WARREN

If you yourself are at peace, then there is at least some peace in the world.

THOMAS MERTON

We count on God's mercy for our past mistakes, on God's love for our present needs, on God's sovereignty for our future.

ST. AUGUSTINE

Whenever I feel fearful emotions overtaking me, I just close my eyes and thank God that He is still on the throne reigning over everything and I take comfort in His control over the affairs of my life.

JOHN WESLEY

FOR FURTHER REFLECTION

Psalm 69:16; Isaiah 9:6–7; 12:2;
Matthew 8:23–27; John 16:33

Today's Prayer

Savior, I desperately need your peace, courage, and strength. My load feels heavy and my heart is heavier still. Help me trust you. Amen.

The Light of God's Word

Your word is a lamp for my feet,
and a light on my path.

PSALM 119:105

Seekers of information often turn to Google when they need help. They just type in a few keywords, and voilà! Thousands of results fill the screen. It's amazing how—in just a couple of decades—we have grown so reliant on the internet for all sorts of assistance.

In Christ, we have a much more reliable and practical source of help than any search engine on our computers or phones. God gave his Word to instruct, convict, challenge, inspire, and encourage us. When our way gets dark, God's Word shines truth into our circumstances, bolstering our faith. Not only that, but in Ephesians 6:17, Paul called the Bible "the sword of the Spirit." When we claim God's Word, we can destroy the lies of the enemy and beat back fear. The Bible is living, active, and powerful.

Do you spend time meditating on and studying the Bible daily? If so, you know the immense and timely help it gives. If not, you can start today. The psalms are especially meaningful during times of distress. Let God's Word wash over your wounded places and refresh your weary soul. You won't regret it!

In darkness God's truth shines most clear.

Corrie ten Boom

It is a pity that many Christians have the TV schedule better memorized than a single chapter from God's precious Word.

Charles Swindoll

As you study your Bible with the help of the Holy Spirit, and live out the truths that God reveals to you, you will discover new stability, strength, and confidence.

Kay Arthur

For Further Reflection

Deuteronomy 8:3; 2 Samuel 22:31;
Psalms 19:7-14; 119:11, 130

Today's Prayer

Lord, thank you for the precious gift of your eternal Word, which lights my way. Forgive me for neglecting it and turning to other things instead.
Amen.

Where Is Your Hope?

Yes, my soul, find rest in God;
my hope comes from him.

PSALM 62:5

D o you hope for a new car, a bigger house, better health, a higher-paying job, a slew of grandkids? Hope is often accompanied by joy. After all, when we imagine a long-held goal or dream being accomplished, we are sure we will be happy.

However, humans are fickle creatures, and the finish line of our contentment keeps moving further and further away. Our sense of pride in a job well done tends to fade quickly, and there is always something else to wish for.

That's why it's important for us to put our fondest hopes and most zealous actions toward the things of God. When we pray, let's pray for as many spiritual blessings as we do physical blessings. Let's praise God as much as we petition him. And let's thank him for the answers he has already given, instead of reciting a litany of requests.

Hope in God, not just the things he can do. Then your hopes will find eternal pleasure and fulfillment that only he can provide.

With God life is an endless hope. Without God, life is a hopeless end.

BILL BRIGHT

Hope is the music of the whole Bible, the heartbeat, the pulse and the atmosphere of the whole Bible.

A. W. Tozer

Our world today so desperately hungers for hope, yet uncounted people have almost given up. There is despair and hopelessness on every hand. Let us be faithful in proclaiming the hope that is in Jesus.

Billy Graham

For Further Reflection

Psalms 25:3; 42:5; 71:14;
Isaiah 40:31; 1 Timothy 6:17

Today's Prayer

Father, I confess that I often put my hope in what the world can offer. Yet I know nothing else but you will satisfy my hungry soul. Starting today, help me place all my hope in you. Amen.

DAY 8

Words That Heal

*Gracious words are a honeycomb, sweet
to the soul and healing to the bones.*

PROVERBS 16:24

Many of our painful memories come from the things people have said to or about us. The old cliché "Sticks and stones may break my bones, but words will never hurt me" is simply untrue. Harsh words can leave deep scars and affect us negatively for years.

In addition, the enemy of our souls loves to remind us of those old wounds—and whisper new lies into our ears. He tells us we're too inexperienced, too broken, too much this or too little that. He shows us others who, we are persuaded to believe, are more skilled or more "together" than we are. He makes us feel discontented and discouraged.

Still . . . if words can hurt, they can also heal. The right words spoken at just the right time are a refreshing treat that can fortify us for our journey in life. Also, when we feed ourselves life-giving (and life-changing) Scriptures, the Holy Spirit comes alongside us in ways only the Comforter can. Nourish yourself with the right words. Then speak words of grace and truth to others—and see what a difference you can make in someone else's life.

A word of encouragement from a teacher to a child can change a life. A word of encouragement from a spouse can save a marriage. A word of encouragement from a leader can inspire a person to reach her potential.

JOHN MAXWELL

God is more powerful than anybody's past, no matter how wretched. He can make us forget—not by erasing the memory but by taking the sting and paralyzing effect out of it.

JIM CYMBALA

I would go to the deeps a hundred times to cheer a downcast spirit. It is good for me to have been afflicted, that I might know how to speak a word in season to one that is weary.

C. H. SPURGEON

FOR FURTHER REFLECTION

Psalm 37:30; Proverbs 18:21;
Matthew 12:37; James 3:10

Today's Prayer

Holy Spirit, thank you for your whispers of truth and comfort. Give me both grace to forgive the people who've spoken harsh words to me and strength to resist the devil's lies. Amen.

DAY 9

Jehovah-Rapha, Our Healer

*If you listen carefully to the Lord your God and do
what is right in his eyes, if you pay attention to
his commands and keep all his decrees, I will not
bring on you any of the diseases I brought on the
Egyptians, for I am the Lord, who heals you.*

EXODUS 15:26

There are many different names for God in the
Bible. One of the most comforting is *Jehovah-Rapha*, a Hebrew name that means "the Lord
who heals." This name was used when the Israelites
were wandering in the wilderness. Moses had taken the
children of Israel into the Desert of Shur, and they had
journeyed for three days without finding any water. When
they finally did find water, they could not drink it. They
called the water Marah, which meant "bitter." The worn-out and thirsty people grumbled about their tribulations,
revealing a root of bitterness in their spirit. Good leader
that he was, Moses prayed. Obeying an instruction from
the Lord, Moses tossed a stick into the water, and it
became fit to drink (or "healed").

The name used for God in this instance was Jehovah-Rapha. The beautiful thing is that God isn't just able to
"heal" water; he also heals people.

Call on the God who heals to heal *you* as he sees fit.

Christ came to bring healing to those who are spiritually sick; you say that you are perfectly well, so you must go your own way, and Christ will go in another direction— towards sinners.

C. H. SPURGEON

Christ is the Good Physician. There is no disease He cannot heal; no sin He cannot remove; no trouble He cannot help. He is the Balm of Gilead, the Great Physician who has never yet failed to heal all the spiritual maladies of every soul that has come unto Him in faith and prayer.

JAMES H. AUGHEY

How sweet the name of Jesus sounds, in a believer's ear! / It soothes his sorrows, heals his wounds, and drives away his fear.

JOHN NEWTON

FOR FURTHER REFLECTION

Psalms 34:18; 147:3; Jeremiah 17:14;
Matthew 9:35; Hebrews 10:22

Today's Prayer

Jehovah-Rapha, I believe your power and provision can transform my life. I ask you in faith to bring the healing I need. Help me submit to your instruction as Moses did and not become bitter about the things I can't change or don't understand. Amen.

A Man of Suffering

*He was despised and rejected by mankind, a man
of suffering, and familiar with pain. Like one from
whom people hide their faces he was despised,
and we held him in low esteem.*

ISAIAH 53:3

Has depression descended on you? If so, know that you are not alone. Several biblical figures—including the prophet Elijah and King David—struggled at times with despair. Many of the psalms paint an unflinching portrait of the up-and-down emotions felt by those who were attacked, maligned, or abandoned.

Even the perfect Son of God experienced deep grief. In the garden of Gethsemane, Jesus groaned under the weight of his dire circumstances and asked God for a way out of his situation. In fact, some Bible translations record that Jesus was so distressed that "his sweat was like drops of blood falling to the ground" (Luke 22:44).

Think about it: our Savior, who was fully human as well as fully God, felt such emotional pain that his body nearly collapsed. Our Savior, who left heaven for you and me, submitted to the torture of the cross out of a love so huge we can't even describe it adequately.

The Man of Sorrows took on our sin. And his love knows no bounds. Ask him to enter your suffering with you. His touch can bring light to dark days that have seemed endless and healing to wounds you've long thought permanent.

When we sin and mess up our lives, we find that God doesn't go off and leave us—he enters into our trouble and saves us.

EUGENE PETERSON

God's purpose at the cross was as real as was the guilt of the crucifiers.

J. I. PACKER

You must submit to supreme suffering in order to discover the completion of joy.

JOHN CALVIN

FOR FURTHER REFLECTION

Psalms 18:28; 103:2-4; Matthew 20:28;
John 3:16; Acts 17:24-25

Today's Prayer

Precious Jesus, "Thank you" doesn't seem enough, but I'll never stop saying it. You left glory and riches to rescue me from eternal separation from God, so now I ask you to take away my feelings of despair and cleanse me from my sins. Heal me, as only you can. Amen.

Joy Will Come

*For you who revere my name, the sun of righteousness
will rise with healing in its rays. And you will go out
and frolic like well-fed calves.*

MALACHI 4:2

Have you ever seen calves frolicking in a pasture? It's quite a sight. They appear to have no sense of time passing or any worry; they play and skip like the youngsters they are. This is the word picture the prophet Malachi painted for God's children in today's verse.

Think of children playing in a sprinkler. They laugh and scream, content to get soaked and not caring whether they are being judged. Their joy is contagious. What a great way to live! Too often when we mature, we leave joy behind. We think being serious about our faith means being serious much of the time. Or perhaps we'd love to live in joy but feel completely beaten down by life's circumstances. Joy seems like a distant dream or a quaint relic of the past.

Our Father longs to help and heal you. His plans for you are perfect and loving, even if things don't feel that way at the moment.

Hold on to hope by committing to believe God is good. Rehearse the truths of Scripture each day (even each hour if you need to), and ask God for mercy and grace—he loves to help his children in their time of need.

One day, in the not-too-distant future, your healing will rise, and your joy will be full.

Make the determination to abide in Jesus wherever you are now or wherever you may be placed in the future.

OSWALD CHAMBERS

I can focus on what's broken and wonder where God is or I can sit in the companionship of Christ who suffered for us and worship him in the middle of the mess. That gives my pain meaning and context.

SHEILA WALSH

Faith is like a tender plant, rooted in Christ alone, watered by the Spirit and the Word, strengthened by the winds of adversity and the sunshine of blessing.

ANNE GRAHAM LOTZ

FOR FURTHER REFLECTION

Psalms 16:11; 30:11; Proverbs 23:18;
Jeremiah 29:11; John 10:10

Today's Prayer

Lord, sometimes I doubt that my healing will come. Thank you for the truths in Scripture and the knowledge that you have amazing plans in place for me. Help me in my times of unbelief. Amen.

God Gives Laughter

Our mouths were filled with laughter, our tongues
with songs of joy. Then it was said among the nations,
"The LORD has done great things for them."

PSALM 126:2

Friend, how long has it been since you experienced a good, hearty laugh (not a chuckle, mind you—a deep, ferocious belly laugh where you almost couldn't catch your breath)? If it's been longer than a day, then it's been too long.

Laughter is a gift from God. As someone once said: "Laughter is the hand of God on the shoulder of a troubled world." In fact, studies have proven a good dose of humor can help speed the healing process. As Solomon wrote in Proverbs 17:22: "A cheerful heart is good medicine." Think about the last time you were with friends or loved ones and someone told a great joke or related a hilarious story. Didn't your mood immediately lift? For the rest of the day, you probably felt lighter and a bit less stressed.

Of course, some personality types find laughter easier to come by than others. If you lean toward the melancholy end of the spectrum, try to surround yourself with cheerful people. You can read lighthearted books, watch funny shows, or listen to clean comedy podcasts. It's not unrealistic or "pie in the sky" to add humor to your days. Rather, it's a life skill that even the wisest man in the world, Solomon, advised his readers to learn.

Humor is a prelude to faith and laughter is the beginning of prayer.

Reinhold Niebuhr

Lighten up and learn to laugh at yourself. Sometimes, being your own source of comedy is the most fun of all.

Luci Swindoll

If the earth is fit for laughter then surely heaven is filled with it. Heaven is the birthplace of laughter.

Martin Luther

For Further Reflection

Genesis 21:6; Job 8:21;
Psalm 100:1-2; Proverbs 15:13, 15

Today's Prayer

Gracious Father, I praise you for the gift of laughter. It helps my mind, body, and soul. Help me to take myself less seriously, at least some of the time.
Amen.

Healing in Community

If it is possible, as far as it depends on you,
live at peace with everyone.

ROMANS 12:18

L et's be honest: sometimes when we are suffering from grief or illness, people in our circle say hurtful things. They give inappropriate or impractical advice, quote Scripture at the wrong time, or minimize our situation. So we tend to shy away from the company of these people.

It's also possible that we've isolated ourselves from the body of Christ because we have cherished our wounds or nursed our grudges. It's easy to do, because we tend to shrink inward when we feel pain. It's counterintuitive for most of us to seek community in times of anguish. Instead, we pull back in self-protection.

Avoiding these tendencies doesn't mean we should fake emotions, rush our progress through the stages of grief, or not take time to heal from whatever we are suffering from. Rather, as we spend time with the Lord each day, we should pray for our hearts to remain soft and to avoid becoming bitter and cynical.

Today, pay attention to the little ways you may have built walls around your heart. Ask God to make you aware of any actions or attitudes that might have taken you away from those who might serve you (and those whom you might serve).

A Christian fellowship lives and exists by the intercession of its members for one another, or it collapses. I can no longer condemn or hate a brother for whom I pray, no matter how much trouble he causes me. His face, that hitherto may have been strange and intolerable to me, is transformed in intercession into the countenance of a brother for whom Christ died, the face of a forgiven sinner.

Dietrich Bonhoeffer

Fellowship is a place of grace, where mistakes aren't rubbed in but rubbed out. Fellowship happens when mercy wins over justice.

Rick Warren

For Further Reflection

Mark 9:50; Ephesians 4:31;
Hebrews 10:24–25; 12:15; 1 John 1:7

Today's Prayer

Heavenly Father, I confess my tendency to cut myself off from others when I am in pain. I repent of any anger, grudge, or bitterness I've held on to. Help me peel off any self-protective layers and show me small ways to launch back into fellowship. Amen.

Sharing the Source of Healing

Is there no balm in Gilead? Is there no physician there? Why then is there no healing for the wound of my people?

JEREMIAH 8:22

When we see or experience devastation, we naturally desire wholeness to return. Our hearts long for heaven, not hell on earth, because we were made for the eternal city. After an earthquake or other natural disaster, compassionate folks rightly rush to help with money, goods, or service. When someone we know has a health problem or loses a loved one, we give them food, flowers, or our time. Those are all good ways to help people, but what about the other aspect of dealing with devastation?

Have you ever wondered why we are not as quick to rush to someone's spiritual aid? We say "I'll pray for you," but we often fail to point to Jesus as the ultimate Healer. The next time you see someone in anguish after a tragedy, remember that as much as they may need physical help, they also might be in spiritual need. Consider what words and actions may help a sufferer move toward our Lord and Savior, rather than away from him. What can you do to point someone toward the ultimate Healer?

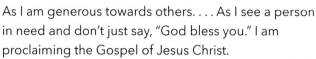

As I am generous towards others. . . . As I see a person in need and don't just say, "God bless you." I am proclaiming the Gospel of Jesus Christ.

Kay Arthur

Rest in this—it is His business to lead, command, impel, send, call. . . . It is your business to obey, follow, move, respond.

Jim Elliot

God can certainly use natural disasters to speak to us— just as He can use other difficulties and tragedies to turn our hearts toward Him.

Billy Graham

For Further Reflection

Isaiah 25:8-9; 43:2; 55:8-9;
Romans 8:28; 1 Peter 3:15

Today's Prayer

Creator of all, forgive me for staying silent when I could have been an instrument in someone else's spiritual healing. Give me opportunities to witness to your grace and power, and grant me strength and faith to obey your call. Amen.

Why Does God Allow Suffering?

Now for a little while you may have had to suffer
grief in all kinds of trials. These have come so that
the proven genuineness of your faith—of greater worth
than gold, which perishes even though refined by fire—
may result in praise, glory and honor
when Jesus Christ is revealed.

1 PETER 1:6–7

There is one basic question about suffering that many believers have: Why does God allow suffering? During Jesus' ministry, his disciples struggled with similar thoughts. When they saw a man blind from birth, they sought answers. "Did this man sin, or did his parents sin?" they asked Jesus.

"'Neither this man nor his parents sinned,' said Jesus, 'but this happened so that the works of God might be displayed in him'" (John 9:3). Jesus then testified to being the light of the world and healed the man. The man went on to share his miraculous story with others.

We learn from this story that God often works through hardship to bring glory to himself. And Peter echoed this sentiment in today's Scripture. Today, ask God to show you how you can use your own problems and your faith to shine his light on other people and bring glory and honor to him.

To choose suffering makes no sense at all; to choose God's will in the midst of our suffering makes all the sense in the world.

OSWALD CHAMBERS

We are told repeatedly in Scripture to prepare for hardships; so why do we believe our lives should be characterized by ease?

PATSY CLAIRMONT

The kingdom of God is a kingdom of paradox, where through the ugly defeat of a cross, a holy God is utterly glorified. Victory comes through defeat; healing through brokenness; finding self through losing self.

CHUCK COLSON

FOR FURTHER REFLECTION

Isaiah 48:10; Zechariah 13:9;
2 Corinthians 4:17–18; Hebrews 12:11

Today's Prayer

Father, you know I have many questions about suffering. But right now, I choose to lay them down and trust what you are doing. Refine my heart through difficult times, and let your light shine through me. Amen.

God Will Sustain You

Even to your old age and gray hairs I am he, I am he who will sustain you. I have made you and I will carry you; I will sustain you and I will rescue you.

ISAIAH 46:4

We have a sustaining God. No matter what our circumstances are, he has promised to be with us and take care of us. We also have a carrying God. When our bodies are tired and our minds are weak, he is willing to hold us in his arms and give us his strength. This is summed up in a poem Warren Wiersbe received from a friend:

> Yesterday God helped me,
> Today He'll do the same.
> How long will this continue?
> Forever—praise His name!

Far too often, however, we try to carry our burdens ourselves, instead of surrendering them to God. Do we think we can do a better job of managing our lives than the Creator of the universe? Our hubris places a barrier between us and him, and our attempts to control and manipulate the things and people in our lives too often result in problems (at least) or disasters (at worst).

Think about the areas in your life where you continue to try and wrest control. Confess your pride to the Lord. Ask him to help you let go. Thank him for his sustaining grace. Then note how much better it feels to give your problems to your strong, dependable Father.

Never think that you can live to God by your own power or strength; but always look to and rely on him for assistance, yea, for all strength and grace.

DAVID BRAINERD

Deny your weakness, and you will never realize God's strength in you.

JONI EARECKSON TADA

There's only one power in the world great enough to help us rise above the difficult things we face: the power of God.

STORMIE OMARTIAN

FOR FURTHER REFLECTION

Psalms 18:35; 55:22; 89:21;
Jeremiah 32:27; Hebrews 1:3

Today's Prayer

Father, you are dependable and strong. Today, I confess I too often try to manage my own life. Now I once again give you my worries and my fears. Sustain me and strengthen me. Amen.

Our Great Hope

Though he slay me, yet will I hope in him.

Job 13:15

In April 2008, twenty-four-year-old Katherine Wolf was a happy new mom with a law student husband. She modeled for extra money and took joy in her family, church community, and her relationship with God. Then one fateful afternoon, a brain stem stroke left her on life support for forty days. She spent the next two years in rehab and underwent numerous surgeries for various issues.

Today, although Katherine walks with a limp, speaks with a slur, and is on permanent disability, she and her husband, Jay, travel the world ministering together. Miraculously, the couple was able to have another child; and though the stroke impacted them financially, physically, and emotionally, the Wolfs have determined to let God use their story of healing and hope for his glory.

In the Wolfs' book *Hope Heals: A True Story of Overwhelming Loss and an Overcoming Love*, Jay wrote, "Yet no matter the origin of the suffering, God's presence remains the same. He finds us in our hurts, if we want to be found. His power to filter the worst that life has to offer, with goodness remaining, is our great hope."

The next time you're tempted to feel hopeless, look for the presence of God in your life—and cling to God's words of hope.

Sometimes our Lord comes with a miracle. . . . Sometimes He simply gives us the grace to face the difficulties of life.

KATHY TROCCOLI

God doesn't squander people's time. He doesn't ignore their pain. He brings not only healing but growth out of even the worst experiences.

HENRY AND RICHARD BLACKABY

Blue skies or dark night, one truth still holds: God has you. And this is the promise He has made to you: He will never let you go.

ANGELA THOMAS

FOR FURTHER REFLECTION

Psalms 25:5; 42:11; 119:49–50, 71;
Ecclesiastes 9:4; Romans 15:13

Today's Prayer

Jesus, thank you for finding me in my hurts. My heart hopes in you, for you alone have the power to turn my situation around and use it for your glory. Amen.

The Upside of Serving

Then your light will break forth like the dawn,
and your healing will quickly appear; then your
righteousness will go before you, and the glory
of the LORD will be your rear guard.

ISAIAH 58:8

I saiah said the words of today's Scripture when he preached to Israel about acts of faith in service to others. He told the children of Israel that to find healing as a nation, they must first confess their sins and get out and serve others, especially the oppressed. When they did that, Isaiah said, God's glory would be revealed, and they would experience healing.

It's easy to focus inward when we are not yet healed. Yet one of the most effective actions we can take during those times is simple: reach out.

Serving gets us out of our own way. Whether we're mowing an elderly neighbor's lawn, painting senior citizens' fingernails at a retirement home, or simply cooking our family a special meal, we are able to focus somewhere else besides our own troubles and sorrows. And that is good for us.

If you're low on energy or time, don't fret: service doesn't have to be big to be effective. Even small steps add up: send a get-well card, shovel someone's sidewalk, make an I-just-wanted-to-see-how-you're-doing phone call, or give someone a compliment. You just might make the other person's day—and yours!

Spread love everywhere you go. Let no one ever come to you without leaving happier.

MOTHER TERESA

The only way you can serve God is by serving other people.

RICK WARREN

Remember that nothing is small in the eyes of God. Do all that you do with love.

ST. THÉRÈSE OF LISIEUX

FOR FURTHER REFLECTION

Mark 10:45; Romans 15:17; Colossians 3:23;
Hebrews 6:10; 1 Peter 4:10

Today's Prayer

God, forgive me for focusing inward too often.
Give me creative ideas and timely reminders
about serving others—and grant me grace
to follow through. Amen.

Resist Self-Pity

Everything that was written in the past was written to teach us, so that through the endurance taught in the Scriptures and the encouragement they provide we might have hope.

ROMANS 15:4

Satan knows our weaknesses and exploits them. One of the biggest temptations we face during the healing process is feeling sorry for ourselves. Satan whispers to us that we are entitled to feel self-pity whenever we experience a painful day or a setback, compare our story with others' journeys, or speculate that God may be taking too long to answer our oft-repeated requests.

When we hear those whispers, the best course of action is to refute them. Instead of listening to the devil's lies, we need to recognize what they are: false. Then we must replace the lies with biblical truth. Scripture is our God-provided, living, and active weapon. We can repeat Scriptures we've memorized, or we can read appropriate verses in our Bibles, and we will win the battle over our minds.

Know this: spiritual warfare is real, but you can win—with the Lord's help. And each time you resist Satan, you get stronger and more mature in your faith.

Readers are advised to remember that the devil is a liar.

C. S. LEWIS

You must hand yourself and all your inward experiences, your temptations, your temperament, your frames and feelings, all over into the care and keeping of your God, and leave them there. He made you, and therefore He understands you and knows how to manage you, and you must trust Him to do it.

Hannah Whitall Smith

"It is written." Stand upon it, and if the devil were fifty devils in one, he could not overcome you. On the other hand, if you leave "It is written," Satan knows more about reasoning than you do. He is far older, has studied mankind very thoroughly, and knows all our weak points. Therefore, the contest will be an unequal one. Do not argue with him but wave in his face the banner of God's Word. Satan cannot endure the infallible truth, for it is death to the falsehood of which he is the father.

C. H. Spurgeon

For Further Reflection

Psalm 119:114; John 15:7;
1 Corinthians 10:13; James 4:7

Today's Prayer

Father, thank you for the Word, which is my sword. Grant me the wisdom to study it, memorize it, and wield it whenever Satan tries to make me feel sorry for myself. Amen.

The Healing Two-Step

He gives strength to the weary and
increases the power of the weak.

Isaiah 40:29

Healing is most often a process, not a one-time event. Even if God chooses to miraculously heal us in a moment, we will still have to deal with emotions and memories from our painful past. And often, healing is a "two steps forward, one step back" journey.

On a practical level, this means that behaviors and attitudes we thought we had left behind will occasionally rear their ugly heads again. If we are struggling to recover after an injury, we may have setbacks and roadblocks we didn't anticipate. During these times, our attempts to find wholeness can seem never-ending. We crave an end to the struggle and are simply exhausted.

When we find ourselves going backward, it would be easy to give up and give in. But rest assured, God does not want us to do that.

If you are in a one-step-back moment, take heart. The ultimate Healer is still with you, and you *are* making progress. Although you are tired, he is not. He loves you with an everlasting love and will uplift and uphold you. Rest in his arms, and take comfort in his presence.

God not only orders our steps, He orders our stops.

GEORGE MÜLLER

When your spirit is heavy, when your heart is broken, when your burdens seem unbearable–trust Him. Look to Him.

ANNE GRAHAM LOTZ

The principle part of faith is patience.

GEORGE MACDONALD

FOR FURTHER REFLECTION

Psalm 68:19; Isaiah 40:27-28;
Matthew 11:28-30; Ephesians 3:16

Today's Prayer

God, I am weary of this uphill battle. Give me strength to keep going and encouragement that my efforts are not in vain. Thank you for your presence. Amen.

Thanking the Great Physician

*One of them, when he saw he was healed,
came back, praising God in a loud voice.*

LUKE 17:15

According to the seventeenth chapter of Luke, Jesus was on his way to Jerusalem when he was seen by ten men with leprosy. They shouted at him, "Have pity on us!" (Luke 17:13). Jesus instructed them to go show themselves to the priest, and on their way, they were healed. Only one of the men, however, came back to thank Jesus for the miracle. As the former leper walked back to the Great Physician, he loudly praised God. He then fell at Jesus' feet and expressed his gratitude. And Jesus asked, "Where are the other nine?" (Luke 17:17).

It's so easy to pray and then forget to thank God when we receive answers: the right medicine, the perfect doctor, a godly counselor, or complete and total healing. We suddenly feel better, and we forget our desperation to find relief.

Let's not be like the other nine. Today, sincerely thank God for the ways he has shown mercy to you. And as you go about your life, find ways to praise God—in front of others—for his answers.

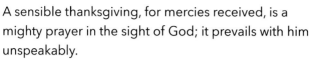

A sensible thanksgiving, for mercies received, is a mighty prayer in the sight of God; it prevails with him unspeakably.

John Bunyan

Jesus does not demand great actions from us, but simply surrender and gratitude.

St. Thérèse of Lisieux

When it comes to life the critical thing is whether you take things for granted or take them with gratitude.

G. K. Chesterton

For Further Reflection

1 Chronicles 16:34; Psalms 9:1; 100:4; 106:1;
Colossians 2:6-7

Today's Prayer

Great Physician, I am sorry for the times I've neglected to thank you for answering my prayers. You are so gracious and forgiving. Thank you for the ways you continue to meet my needs. Amen.

Don't Be Afraid of Silence

*Tremble and do not sin; when you are on your beds,
search your hearts and be silent.*

PSALM 4:4

God's people need silence to cultivate a relationship with him. We also need silence if we're to truly heal from the ways life wounds us. If we only speak and never listen, we won't be able to discern what God wants us to do next. If we are always surrounded by sound, we may not be able to hear the Spirit's nudge to forgive someone or let go of our grievances.

Of course, we're often simply afraid to hear from God—afraid that he'll require too much of us or ask us to do something we don't want to do. It's easier to live on autopilot and keep our days full than to silence our souls and tune in to his wavelength.

The next time you feel yourself hesitating to get quiet before the Lord, remember that God's plans for us are perfect. He knows what's best, and he equips us for anything he calls us to. All his ways lead, in the end, to abundant joy.

Silence does good to the soul.

ST. THÉRÈSE OF LISIEUX

Somewhere we know that without silence, words lose their meaning.

Henri Nouwen

God is the friend of silence. See how nature—trees, flowers, grass—grows in silence; see the stars, the moon and the sun, how they move in silence. . . . We need silence to be able to touch souls.

Mother Teresa

The silence that makes it possible to hear God speak also makes it possible for us to hear the world's words for what they really are—tinny and unconvincing lies.

Eugene Peterson

For Further Reflection

Psalm 46:10; Proverbs 17:28;
Habakkuk 2:20; John 10:27

Today's Prayer

Lord, too often I fill every moment with noise and commotion. Remind me to quiet my soul before you so that I can hear you and follow your path toward healing. Amen.

DAY 23

Waiting for Healing

Wait for the Lord; be strong and take heart
and wait for the Lord.

Psalm 27:14

When God doesn't answer your prayers for healing right away, how do you react? What do you think and feel? (Be honest!) Many of us feel hurt, angry, or confused. After all, healing is a good thing. Why wouldn't God want us to experience it as soon as possible? We then look around at others he has healed and wonder if he is unhappy with us. And often, we become unhappy with him.

After all, none of us really likes to wait. We have instant rice, Instant Pots, and almost-instant Amazon deliveries. Thanks to our ever-present smartphones, we can look up any information we need in a split second. None of those things make it easier for us to have patience.

What's an impatient believer to do? First, since forbearance (often translated as patience) is a fruit of the Spirit (Galatians 5:22–23), we must ask God to cultivate it within us—and ask him how we can come alongside him in that regard. We also need to note the times and places in which we feel impatient and then ask ourselves why we feel that way. Are we seeking to control something we can't? Are we letting our flesh take over, instead of walking in the Spirit? Finally, we can be aware of the small ways God is working so that we don't focus only on the big answers.

We shall not grow weary of waiting upon God if we remember how long and how graciously He once waited for us.

C. H. SPURGEON

Waiting on God requires the willingness to bear uncertainty, to carry within oneself the unanswered question, lifting the heart to God about it whenever it intrudes upon one's thoughts.

ELISABETH ELLIOT

If you're waiting with God, waiting is okay. If you're always waiting *on* God, you'll be frustrated. God never seems to work at the speed that we want Him to.

LOUIE GIGLIO

FOR FURTHER REFLECTION

Psalm 37:7; Proverbs 14:29; Isaiah 30:18;
Micah 7:7; Colossians 3:12

Today's Prayer

Father, forgive me for being impatient with your timing and ways. I want to be more like you. Please show me the ways in which I can help you cultivate this fruit of the Spirit within me. And thank you for the ways you are already answering my prayers.
Amen.

A Chance to Surrender

Therefore, I urge you, brothers and sisters, in view of
God's mercy, to offer your bodies as a living sacrifice,
holy and pleasing to God—this is your true
and proper worship.

ROMANS 12:1

Many of us—especially those of us who tend to be Type A personalities—are addicted to the illusion of control. In our daily lives, we attempt to control our calendar, activities, and environment. However, it only takes one traffic jam or long line at the store to alter our schedules and remind us that we're not in control at all. Not really.

If we sit with that realization too long, we can become full of anxiety and fear. In our humanness, we may double down on calendar apps and micromanagement techniques, thinking that better tools will give us better control. We might even attempt to control our spiritual lives—by not listening to God or the Holy Spirit, but instead rushing through Bible study and worship and engaging in petition-heavy prayer times.

But look at it this way: the journey from broken to healed holds multiple opportunities to let go and to surrender our desires, relationships, plans, and emotions to the Lord. If we allow him to, he'll use our ailments and hang-ups as spiritual lessons. In the process, he'll bring us to our knees and show us how much we need him. Through it all, he'll graciously teach us more about ourselves—and himself—training us in righteousness.

Won't you give up control to the Lord today? After all, you never really had it in the first place.

We can only learn to know ourselves and do what we can—namely, surrender our will and fulfill God's will in us.

St. Teresa of Ávila

We try to bargain with God . . . I will follow you but don't touch my children, or my husband, don't give me cancer. . . . We are afraid our surrender to God will unleash evil. But evil will come, because evil will come. We live in a broken world.

Kay Warren

In a real sense faith is total surrender to God.

Martin Luther King Jr.

For Further Reflection

Isaiah 64:8; Jeremiah 10:23;
Mark 8:35; Galatians 2:20

Today's Prayer

Father, I so often think I have things under my control, but it's all an illusion. Thank you that you hold everything in your hands. Help me to trust you more. Amen.

Press On toward Healing

Forgetting what is behind and straining toward what is ahead, I press on toward the goal to win the prize for which God has called me heavenward in Christ Jesus.

PHILIPPIANS 3:13–14

In the four gospels, we often see Jesus asking people who come to him for healing, "What do you want me to do for you?" Instead of automatically healing them, he engaged them and made them think and talk about what they deeply desired.

Think about the ways God has worked in your own life. If you've known Jesus as Savior a long time, did your maturity as a believer happen overnight? No. It took time—and discipline. God works with our personalities, talents, and environments to bring us into a place of transformation. And unless we understand and participate in his process, pressing on with endurance and faith, we will not reach the level of wholeness and sanctification he desires for us.

If Jesus were to appear in front of you and ask, "What do you want me to do for you?" what would you say? Think and pray about that (and if you keep a journal, record your thoughts). Then ask the Lord, "What do you want me to do for you?" and listen quietly to what he says. Journal about his answer, too.

The Lord help me to press after God forever.

David Brainerd

The question is: Are you pressing on to make Christ your own? That is, are you resolving day by day to count Christ as your supreme treasure and count everything else as rubbish by comparison?

John Piper

God knows our situation; He will not judge us as if we had no difficulties to overcome. What matters is the sincerity and perseverance of our will to overcome them.

C. S. Lewis

For Further Reflection

Proverbs 16:3; Hosea 6:3;
Philippians 3:10–12; Hebrews 10:36

Today's Prayer

Jesus, I know you desire my freedom and wholeness even more than I do. Transform me from the inside out as I press on toward all you have for me. And help me to work with you, not against you, in the process. Amen.

The Power of Worship

Ascribe to the LORD the glory due his name; bring an offering and come before him. Worship the LORD in the splendor of his holiness.

1 CHRONICLES 16:29

Whether we're experiencing emotionally or physically taxing circumstances, we can get caught up in the daily battle toward health and forget the big picture. Details like juggling appointments, choosing care providers, filling out insurance forms, overcoming setbacks, and dealing with others' comments can drain our energy and leave us bone-tired and world-weary.

In those times, God has provided a gift to calm our hearts and lift our spirits: worship. Heartfelt, genuine worship brings us into God's presence faster than almost anything else. It gets our minds off our ever-changing circumstances and onto our never-changing God.

We can worship God by reciting Scriptures, praying spontaneous or written prayers, or using praise music. If you don't have a favorite worship musician, ask Christian friends to recommend a few artists you can listen to. Purchase CDs to listen to or download songs that encourage and energize you. Listen to the music regularly as a pathway to the Father. Soon enough, you'll probably find yourself humming along—and lifting your hands.

No matter how you choose to worship God, go to him every day and rely on his mighty power.

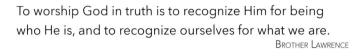

To worship God in truth is to recognize Him for being who He is, and to recognize ourselves for what we are.

Brother Lawrence

Worry and worship cannot exist in the same space. One always displaces the other. Choose worship.

Louie Giglio

Life is filled with things you don't expect, but the Bible tells us to respond by trusting God and continuing to worship him.

Laura Story

For Further Reflection

Nehemiah 9:6; Psalms 95:6; 150:1-6; John 4:24

Today's Prayer

Lord, thank you for the gift of worship. I confess I neglect this gift too often and get caught up in the dailiness of life, instead of the goodness of your grace. Today and all the days that follow, I will worship you in all your glory, and I will praise you for your majesty. Amen.

God's Word Gives Healing

*My son, pay attention to what I say; turn your ear
to my words. Do not let them out of your sight, keep
them within your heart; for they are life to those who
find them and health to one's whole body.*

PROVERBS 4:20–22

Solomon, the probable author of today's Scripture, said that his words do not just bring life and healing but that they *are* life and healing to all who find them.

Because Jesus is the Word of God (John 1:1), when we who have accepted Christ meditate on, memorize, study, and repeat Bible passages, we are infused with his life. Instead of letting us believe the lies that Satan has spouted at us (through other people, the media, and culture in general)—such as "You're not good enough" and "God couldn't forgive what you've done!"—God actually uses the power inherent in his Word to re-train our brains. We begin to reject the darkness of the devil's falsehoods as we replace them with the light of God's truth: you and I are beloved children of God, perfect and forgiven in his sight through the power of the resurrected Lord Jesus.

Choose to make God's Word a priority. As you open the Scriptures, ask the Holy Spirit to reveal new truths. Then, as you go about your day, be attentive to ways he wants to infuse you with his life. Test what you are told or think about yourself against the light of the Word. If it's a lie, immediately replace it with a Bible verse.

In this way, we partner with the Trinity to tear down strongholds like perfectionism, addiction, and fear; and our gracious Father begins to heal our thoughts and hearts. What an amazing gift!

We can't really tell how crooked our thinking is until we line it up with the straight edge of Scripture.

ELISABETH ELLIOT

I would say 90 percent of Christians do not have a worldview, in other words a view of the world, based on the Scripture and a relationship with God.

JOSH MCDOWELL

The Bible was not given for our information but for our transformation.

D. L. MOODY

FOR FURTHER REFLECTION

Matthew 4:4; Romans 12:2;
2 Corinthians 3:18; 2 Timothy 3:16

Today's Prayer

Mighty God, thank you for the power of your Word
to transform me. I can't get over it.
I pray I never will. Amen.

DAY 28

Only God Can Heal Us

*Jesus turned and saw her. "Take heart, daughter," he
said, "your faith has healed you." And the woman
was healed at that moment.*

MATTHEW 9:22

Present-day faith healers claim to have special God-given powers that people can access—if they come to ticketed events or give money to the healer's ministry. Thankfully, some of these so-called ministers have been discredited after investigators discovered that the healings had been staged. However, some of these faith healers are still preying on sick people's desperation and despair.

One thing that separates Jesus from such faith healers is the evidence to his power. Not only did he heal people with his words and touch—some from miles away—but he also rose from the dead after being brutally tortured and nailed to a wooden cross.

And because he is still alive, seated at the right hand of the Father in heaven, he's still in the healing business. Do we spend as much time seeking after him as we do seeking man-made "miracle" cures and treatments? Our bodies are temporal, while our spirits are eternal. Someday, we will shed this earthly frame and live with him forever. Not only can we have eternal life one day, we can have abundant life today—whether we're fully healed yet or not.

Only God can fully heal us—body, soul, *and* spirit. Trust him to do so in your own life.

The Church possesses in Jesus, our Divine Healer, an inestimable treasure, which she does not yet know how to appreciate.

Andrew Murray

God's specialty is raising dead things to life and making impossible things possible. You don't have the need that exceeds His power.

Beth Moore

Jesus has come to redeem where it is wrong and heal the world where it is broken. His miracles are not just proofs that he has power but also wonderful foretastes of what he is going to do with that power. Jesus' miracles are not just a challenge to our minds, but a promise to our hearts, that the world we all want is coming.

Tim Keller

For Further Reflection

Psalm 40:5; Matthew 8:13; Luke 6:17-19;
John 11:38-44; Acts 3:16

Today's Prayer

Jesus, I want to know you more. I praise you for your healing power! I know that you—and you alone—have the power to fully heal me. Please restore every part of me, in your holy and precious name. Amen.

When Anxiety Threatens

Do not be anxious about anything, but in every situation, by prayer and petition, with thanksgiving, present your requests to God.

PHILIPPIANS 4:6

J esus told us in no uncertain terms that believers are *not* to worry. But that command seems laughable! How in the world are we to obey it?

In Philippians, which Paul wrote from a jail cell, Christians are instructed to not be anxious but instead to present our requests to God. After we do, his supernatural peace will fill our minds and our hearts through Christ. As someone once said, "The beginning of anxiety is the end of faith, and the beginning of true faith is the end of anxiety."

That's not to say we will never need help in order to leave our fears behind. Some people may require godly counseling or a doctor's help to gain victory over anxiety, especially if their struggle is debilitating. If that description fits your life, ask God to give you wisdom and lead you to people who can assist you in living a normal life.

We are not meant to worry about everything all the time. The world rests on God's shoulders, so place your cares on him and rest in his grace.

This much is sure: It's not God's will that you lead a life of perpetual anxiety. It's not his will that you face every day with dread and trepidation.

Max Lucado

As you walk through the valley of the unknown, you will find the footprints of Jesus both in front of you and beside you.

Charles Stanley

What else does anxiety about the future bring you but sorrow upon sorrow?

Thomas à Kempis

For Further Reflection

Psalm 139:23–24; Isaiah 41:10;
Matthew 6:25–34; Luke 8:22–25

Today's Prayer

Savior, calm my anxious heart. Help me place my worries at your feet—and not take them back. Amen.

Glorifying God in Weakness

*Whatever you do, whether in word or deed, do it all in
the name of the Lord Jesus, giving thanks
to God the Father through him.*

COLOSSIANS 3:17

O ne of the key teachings of the Christian faith
is that in whatever we do—work, play, rest, eat,
drink—we should seek to glorify God. Thus,
our lives, not just our words, will be a testimony to his
saving love and grace. But those who are suffering from
long-term or chronic ailments might wonder: "How can
I glorify God in this? Surely, God cannot be praised
through a life of infirmity! Faith is about overcoming and
abundance, not weakness and sickness, right?" Wrong.
Throughout the Bible, God chose people who seemed
too young, too old, too unqualified, too disabled, or too
flawed; and he worked mightily through them. And he can
do the same through you.

As Katherine Wolf, a stroke survivor, wrote in *Hope Heals:
A True Story of Overwhelming Loss and an Overcoming Love*:

> I have learned to do many things well—to wait well,
> suffer well, cope well, persevere well, and even to lose
> well. Our culture tells us to succeed, be beautiful,
> avoid pain, and be happy. What if everything
> important in our lives is actually the opposite?

The very things that we find limiting or frustrating, God
can use. The question is: Will we let him take all the

parts of our lives—including the messy, embarrassing, and painful ones—and implement them for his glory?

Disappointment often focuses on the failure of our own agenda rather than on God's long-term purposes for us, which may use stress and struggle as tools for strengthening our spiritual muscles.

Luci Shaw

Faith is deliberate confidence in the character of God whose ways you may not understand at the time.

Oswald Chambers

Felt weakness deepens dependence on Christ for strength each day. The weaker we feel, the harder we lean.

J. I. Packer

FOR FURTHER REFLECTION

Job 36:5; Psalm 119:67; Isaiah 63:8-9;
1 Corinthians 1:27; 2 Corinthians 12:9-10

Today's Prayer

God, I give you my weaknesses, my failures, and my struggles. Use everything as you will and for your will. Amen.

Keeping the Sabbath

*In six days the LORD made the heavens and the earth,
the sea, and all that is in them, but he rested on the
seventh day. Therefore the LORD blessed
the Sabbath day and made it holy.*

EXODUS 20:11

Without the Sabbath, we can become too hurried and frantic. Those of us in pursuit of wholeness especially need the Sabbath to take a break from the hard work (and roller-coaster nature) of healing.

However, Sabbath is difficult to implement because it is countercultural. We no longer have blue laws, which required that retail establishments be closed on Sunday. Kids' and adults' sports teams practice and have games on Sunday. Even some churches tend not to treat the Sabbath well; they fill up Sundays with services, luncheons, life groups, and meetings. Of course, since Jesus fulfilled the law, legalism is not why (or how!) we should keep the Sabbath. We should do so out of respect for God and the limits he lovingly placed on us as a good, loving "*Abba*, Father" (Mark 14:36; Romans 8:15; Galatians 4:6).

So what is required to keep the Sabbath? Most believers think of two things: worship and rest. Once you've had a taste of true Sabbath—with its peaceful, life-giving flow— you will be committed to keeping it.

After church and lunch, take a nap; then put together a puzzle or play a board game with friends or family. Or watch movies with your family or friends. If you have a work schedule different from Monday through Friday, find another day (or a few hours in the week) to worship God and to just *be*. Your body, mind, and spirit will thank you.

God presents the Sabbath rest as a shelter we can enter.

CHARLES SWINDOLL

Sabbath's golden rule: Cease from what is necessary. Embrace that which gives life.

MARK BUCHANAN

Sabbath is not simply the pause that refreshes. It is the pause that transforms.

WALTER BRUEGGEMANN

FOR FURTHER REFLECTION

Exodus 20:8; Leviticus 19:30;
Mark 2:27; Hebrews 4:9–10

Today's Prayer

Loving Lord, thank you for the gift of the Sabbath. Help me to keep it holy, and show me how to create space in my life, so I may rest from the work you've set in front of me. Amen.

God Delights in You

The Lord your God is with you, the Mighty Warrior
who saves. He will take great delight in you; in his
love he will no longer rebuke you, but
will rejoice over you with singing.

ZEPHANIAH 3:17

Do you believe God looks at you with frustration, disappointment, or condemnation? If so, it will affect everything in your life—including your healing.

The Bible says that God "take[s] great delight in you." Like parents cuddling their children sing lullabies to them and look at them with awestruck devotion and wonder, God sees you as his masterpiece. In Christ, there is no condemnation—no matter your past failures, your annoying quirks, or your present struggles.

Remember that the next time the devil tries to make you believe that you are worthless. As God's child, you can— and should—picture him smiling at you, rejoicing in how you are made. After all, he's the one who made you.

What did Jesus know that enabled him to do what he did? Here's part of the answer. He knew the value of people. He knew that each human being is a treasure. And because he did, people were not a source of stress, but a source of joy.

MAX LUCADO

God reminded me how beautiful we all are to Him, after all, we were created in His own image, and He looks at me, at you, in all our sweat and dirt and brokenness, and says, "I choose you. You are beautiful."

KATIE DAVIS MAJORS

Define yourself radically as one beloved by God. This is the true self. Every other identity is illusion.

BRENNAN MANNING

FOR FURTHER REFLECTION

Genesis 1:26–28, 31; 2 Samuel 22:20;
Psalms 139:14; 149:4; Proverbs 12:22

Today's Prayer

Father, so often I feel condemnation instead of conviction. Forgive me for listening to Satan when he tries to tell me I'm worthless. From now on, I will look to your Word to know my worth. Thank you for delighting in me! Amen.

Trusting God's Timing

In repentance and rest is your salvation,
in quietness and trust is your strength,
but you would have none of it.

ISAIAH 30:15

The children of Israel are examples of what not to do when you're still in the middle of the wilderness—not yet in your promised land. They saw God's miraculous provision over and over again (the parting of the Red Sea, manna and quail, water from a rock—to name just a few), but they quickly forgot those wonders afterward. They even built idols to worship while their leader was communing with God on their behalf (Exodus 32:1-8)!

We're no different, though. We create idols of convenience, content to worship the wrong things. We distract ourselves with material goods, media, or unhealthy relationships in order not to feel too much. And we question God instead of trusting him.

Thankfully, we have the same God who was full of forgiveness and compassion to his chosen people, who brought the Israelites to the promised land, not because of their great love for him but because of his great love for them. Today, ask him for strength and endurance, and confess your tendency to place other things above him. He will bring you out of your wilderness in his perfect timing.

God's timing is always perfect. Trust His delays. He's got you.

TONY EVANS

There are no "ifs" in God's kingdom. . . . His timing is perfect. His will is our hiding place.

CORRIE TEN BOOM

If you refuse to be hurried and pressed, if you stay your soul on God, nothing can keep you from that clearness of spirit which is life and peace. In that stillness you will know what His will is.

AMY CARMICHAEL

FOR FURTHER REFLECTION

Ecclesiastes 3:1, 11; Acts 1:7;
Galatians 4:4; 2 Peter 3:8

Today's Prayer

Lord, give me your endurance to cross this wilderness with faithfulness. Give me your strength to resist the pull of idols. I long to trust you more; thank you for giving me opportunities to do so.
Amen.

Our Hope Is in Heaven

Since ancient times no one has heard, no ear has perceived, no eye has seen any God besides you, who acts on behalf of those who wait for him.

ISAIAH 64:4

This topsy-turvy world provides many opportunities to fear. We fear what the future may bring—a financial meltdown, mental decline, or physical injury. And when we're afraid, we often fall back on the common belief that money will keep us safe. It's natural to crave security, but as believers we know that true security is found in our relationship with God, not in how much we have. True security doesn't depend on our external circumstances.

We can take comfort in knowing our circumstances on earth, as good or bad as they may get, are nothing at all compared to the treasures heaven will have for us. Our desire for health, wealth, and security is really a desire for our ever-constant God, who alone can assuage the deepest longings of our hearts. And whether we ever achieve what we dream of or not, we can rest assured: our dreams here are shallow, gray imitations of our future in the kingdom of God, where we will reign with Jesus and take pleasure eternally in his good gifts.

On bad days, hold on to the hope that heaven provides. On good days, thank God for the glimpses of heaven you see.

You can look forward with hope, because one day there will be no more separation, no more scars, no more suffering in My Father's House. It's the home of your dreams!

ANNE GRAHAM LOTZ

Christians have a dual citizenship—on earth and in heaven—and our citizenship in heaven ought to make us better people here on earth.

WARREN WIERSBE

He whose head is in heaven need not fear to put his feet into the grave.

MATTHEW HENRY

Has this world been so kind to you that you should leave with regret? There are better things ahead than any we leave behind.

C. S. LEWIS

FOR FURTHER REFLECTION

Psalm 8:1; Matthew 6:19-20; 1 Corinthians 2:9-10;
Philippians 3:20-21; Hebrews 11:1

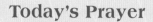

Today's Prayer

Jesus, my heart so often pulls me in ungodly directions. I think if I achieve more, meet the right person, or gain more followers on social media, I will have what my soul craves. Pull me back to your side, where eternal pleasures await. Amen.

Heaven Is Our Lifeblood

I consider that our present sufferings are not worth comparing with the glory that will be revealed in us.

ROMANS 8:18

Heaven is the lifeblood of Christianity. It's the place Jesus came from and will take us back to, and the place we bring others to by sharing his story. Yet so many of us go through our lives with little or no thought about what happens after our earthly death. We spend time instead on daily activities and responsibilities, and that's understandable. However . . .

If we never think of heaven or long for it, we are potentially missing out on all God has for us here. Meditating on eternity spent in the presence of a perfect God, where we will be free from the constraints that bind us, can encourage our hearts and embolden us to share more freely about the hope of Jesus.

Similarly, difficult emotions and experiences can be redeemed when we focus on the eternal home our heart longs for. The next time you feel pain—either emotional or physical—concentrate on the promises in Scripture about heaven and notice how it helps you.

The best we can hope for in this life is a knothole peek at the shining realities ahead. Yet a glimpse is enough. It's enough to convince our hearts that whatever sufferings and sorrows currently assail us aren't worthy of comparison to that which waits over the horizon.

Joni Eareckson Tada

In my travels I have found that those who keep Heaven in view remain serene and cheerful in the darkest day. If the glories of Heaven were more real to us, if we lived less for material things and more for things eternal and spiritual, we would be less easily disturbed by this present life.

Billy Graham

For the Christian, death is not the end of adventure but a doorway from a world where dreams and adventures shrink, to a world where dreams and adventures forever expand.

Randy Alcorn

For Further Reflection

Isaiah 65:17; Daniel 2:44; John 14:1–4;
Revelation 7:16–17

Today's Prayer

Heavenly Father, most days I forget about eternity and instead dwell on the temporary pangs and pains of this life. Give me a fresh, heavenly perspective. Increase my longing to be with you—and bring others along with me—for eternity. Amen.

Training with the Bible

All Scripture is God-breathed and is useful for teaching, rebuking, correcting and training in righteousness, so that the servant of God may be thoroughly equipped for every good work.

2 Timothy 3:16–17

We have a tool for spiritual training that's more powerful than the strongest, fittest, fastest physical athlete: the Bible. Of course, just as athletes can find a multitude of reasons to avoid practice and exercise, we have plenty of ways to distract us from spending time in God's Word: going to work, cleaning the house, firing up the grill to make dinner, going to a child's soccer game, watching a movie—to name just a few of the things that keep us busy. However, there's simply no better resource or instruction manual for us than the Good Book.

Look over your daily schedule and be creative about inserting time to read the Bible. For instance, you could listen to an audio Bible during your commute. You could download Scripture-based sermons and listen to them while you exercise. If you have a favorite verse or passage, work on committing it to memory.

Little by little, you will see real and lasting life change. God promises that—and you can take him at his word.

Ultimately, the goal of personal Bible study is a transformed life and a deep and abiding relationship with Jesus Christ.

KAY ARTHUR

Delighting in God's Word leads us to delight in God, and delight in God drives away fear.

DAVID JEREMIAH

Down through the years, I turned to the Bible and found in it all that I needed.

RUTH BELL GRAHAM

Nothing less than a whole Bible can make a whole Christian.

A. W. TOZER

FOR FURTHER REFLECTION

Psalms 19:7–11; 119:1–8, 169–170;
Matthew 22:29; Luke 24:45

Today's Prayer

Jesus, I praise you because you are the Word made flesh, yet I confess I make excuses not to "train" with you and your words of life. Show me how to make time to study Scripture every day. Amen.

Play Is Healing

*They celebrate your abundant goodness
and joyfully sing of your righteousness.*

PSALM 145:7

Many adults have lost the ability to play. We are too serious and anxious, and it is harming our health and our communities. Instead of engaging in healthy activities like sports, we sit indoors and stare at computer or television screens for hours at a time.

Of course, a well-balanced life can include watching movies and television shows, playing online games, keeping up with current events, and interacting on social media. However, God made our bodies to revel in fresh air, laughter, and movement; and we are not getting enough of any of those. Play is healing.

Stuart Brown, an expert on the value of play, believes that play is as basic a biological need as sleep or food. Maybe that's one of the reasons why Jesus loved little children and encouraged us to come to him like children.

Try to incorporate some form of play into each week: dust off a board game, join a church softball league, sing a favorite song, or take dance lessons. Celebrate God's goodness by doing something fun. Then see how your mood lifts, along with your heart.

Angels can fly because they take themselves lightly. . . .
Satan fell by force of gravity.

G. K. CHESTERTON

If it seems a childish thing to do, do it in remembrance
that you are a child.

FREDERICK BUECHNER

It is requisite for the relaxation of the mind that we make
use, from time to time, of playful deeds and jokes.

THOMAS AQUINAS

FOR FURTHER REFLECTION

2 Samuel 6:14–15; Proverbs 17:22;
Matthew 18:3; Mark 10:13–14

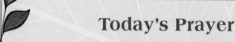

Today's Prayer

God of the cosmos, surely you were playing when
you created the ostrich, kangaroo, and hyena! I
know you want me to have childlike faith. Show me
how to become more like a child again, in all the
best ways. Amen.

Why Healthy Boundaries Matter

*Yet the news about [Jesus] spread all the more, so that
crowds of people came to hear him and to be healed
of their sicknesses. But Jesus often withdrew
to lonely places and prayed.*

LUKE 5:15–16

Healthy boundaries are essential to the process of healing. Most of us learn the wrong way to approach the topic of boundaries, simply because so many of us are part of dysfunctional families. We avoid conflict, love to be liked, and believe "don't rock the boat" is key to having good relationships.

But boundaries are critical if we want to thrive. We need to set limits with our finances (i.e., create a budget), or we'll end up in debt. We sometimes need to say no to our children, or they'll end up spoiled (or hurt). In our personal lives, we must erect healthy boundaries around our eating, work life, and media consumption, or we'll end up out of balance.

In today's verse, we see that when Jesus was preaching to large groups of people and discipling a small group of men, he regularly took time away from others to be with his father (Matthew 14:13, 23; Mark 1:35; Luke 6:12). Ask God to make you aware of the places you've not put up appropriate boundaries—or where you've encroached on the boundaries of others. Then, as he reveals the truth, be willing to make healthier choices.

Boundaries help us keep the good in and the bad out. Setting boundaries inevitably involves taking responsibility for your choices. You are the one who makes them. You are the one who must live with their consequences. And you are the one who may be keeping yourself from making the choices you could be happy with.

HENRY CLOUD AND JOHN TOWNSEND

Love can't rule when shame is in charge.

JOHN TOWNSEND

Taking good care of yourself means the people in your life receive the best of you rather than what is left of you.

LUCILLE ZIMMERMAN

FOR FURTHER REFLECTION

Proverbs 4:23; 22:6; 1 Corinthians 5:11;
Titus 2:11-12

Today's Prayer

Lord, I need your help and strength to set up and keep appropriate boundaries. Too often, I put others' approval ahead of yours. Teach me to be smart and disciplined, so I can move toward enjoying the abundant life you promised. Amen.

DAY 39

Heroes and
Role Models

*All these people were still living by faith
when they died.*

Hebrews 11:13

It's good to have a hero to look up to as you journey toward all God has for you. Role models inspire us to make wise choices and to keep moving forward, despite life's inevitable failures and disappointments. While we shouldn't worship those we consider heroes, we *can* use them as role models.

Scripture is full of heroes (and heroines!): Esther was used by God to save her people; the apostle Peter denied Jesus but ended up becoming a mighty force for God; Ruth sacrificed her own comfort to stay with her mother-in-law and ended up in the lineage of Jesus. And these are just three of the many role models found in the Bible.

Pick one or two heroes in the Bible and study their lives. (Hebrews 11, known as the Faith Hall of Fame, is a great place to start.) Pray as you study, asking God to show you character traits you need to work on. Just remember that no role model—save Jesus—is perfect.

The honesty of Scripture is one of the reasons I knew that the Bible would be the place to go to learn what a real man should be and do.

Dennis Rainey

The mystery is not that an earthly hero can still be flawed and fall to cultural pressures but that God, in His mercy, chooses at times to retain only the snapshots He took when they were standing firm. Then, when students like us flip through the photo album of biblical figures, we can take those moments, if not their entire lives, as beautiful examples.

BETH MOORE

God does not choose men because they are great, but makes them great because He has chosen them.

JONATHAN EDWARDS

All heroes are shadows of Christ.

JOHN PIPER

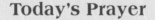

FOR FURTHER REFLECTION

1 Corinthians 11:1; Titus 2:7–8;
Hebrews 11:4–40; 13:7

Today's Prayer

Jesus, thank you for being the ultimate role model. Guide me as I look for traits to admire in others; help me day by day to become the type of person others want to emulate. Amen.

Suffering Well

*We also glory in our sufferings, because we know
that suffering produces perseverance; perseverance,
character; and character, hope.*

ROMANS 5:3–4

D o you consider suffering a privilege? Most of us don't, yet the Bible teaches us that as believers, we should "count it pure joy" to undergo trials (James 1:2). Why? Because our suffering produces perseverance, which leads to character, which then leads to hope.

Perseverance, character, hope—things that we all aspire to. However, not many of us wish to sign up for the course that leads to the diploma. We want the degree without having to go through the difficult process that leads to graduation. We like comfort and happiness, and we don't like to be inconvenienced—let alone refined.

Still, suffering well is a choice God gives us. We can fight against it, becoming angry and even bitter, or we can ask God to transform and purify us through the trials he allows in our lives. The question is: Which path will you and I take?

No man ought to lay a cross upon himself, or to adopt tribulation . . . but if a cross or tribulation come upon him, then let him suffer it patiently, and know that it is good and profitable for him.

MARTIN LUTHER

The greatest Christians in history seem to say that their sufferings ended up bringing them the closest to God—so this is the best thing that could happen, not the worst.

PETER KREEFT

The deepest level of worship is praising God in spite of pain, thanking God during a trial, trusting him when tempted, surrendering while suffering, and loving him when he seems distant.

RICK WARREN

The disciples bear the suffering laid on them only by the power of him who bears all suffering on the cross. As bearers of suffering, they stand in communion with the Crucified.

DIETRICH BONHOEFFER

FOR FURTHER REFLECTION

Deuteronomy 8:2; Psalms 57:1; 66:10;
James 1:2-4; 1 Peter 2:21

Today's Prayer

Lord, I want to learn how to accept suffering as a path to purification. I long to suffer well. Give me grace to see my trials as welcome strangers I meet on the road to spiritual growth. Amen.

DAY 41

When You're Weary

I will refresh the weary and satisfy the faint.

JEREMIAH 31:25

Some days, the climb toward healing can seem too long, too steep, and too lonely. We wonder if we'll ever really be healed. "Isn't healing a mirage?" we ask ourselves. "It seems to disappear just as I get close to it."

Even Jesus—the one perfect God-in-man—felt this way. Because he was fully human as well as fully divine, his feet got tired, his emotions became frayed, and his patience grew thin. Still, he didn't sin. He did, however, keep a line of communication always open to his Father. You might even say he had a red phone to the great throne!

Similarly, we should keep talking to our Lord. When we're too tired to pray or read Scripture, we can whisper, "Lord, have mercy. Jesus, have mercy. Christ, have mercy" (one of the variations of the Jesus Prayer).

Rest assured: when you are bone-tired and ready to give up or give in, your Father knows. He sees. He has already planned to send encouragement and refreshment your way. Watch in expectation to see how he does so.

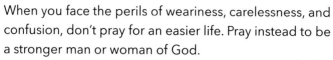

When you face the perils of weariness, carelessness, and confusion, don't pray for an easier life. Pray instead to be a stronger man or woman of God.

LUIS PALAU

We will never know weariness in heaven.

BILLY GRAHAM

Seeing that a pilot steers the ship in which we sail, who will never allow us to perish even in the midst of shipwrecks, there is no reason why our minds should be overwhelmed with fear and overcome with weariness.

JOHN CALVIN

FOR FURTHER REFLECTION

Psalms 51:10; 119:28; Isaiah 50:4; 58:11;
1 Thessalonians 5:17

Today's Prayer

Lord, have mercy. Jesus, have mercy. Christ, have mercy. Amen.

The Importance of Forgiveness

If you do not forgive others their sins,
your Father will not forgive your sins.

MATTHEW 6:15

Unforgiveness is not only detrimental to our spirits, but it can be corrosive to our bodies as well. We've all probably known or at least heard of a person who held on to a grudge so long that it wrecked their relationships and even their health.

As believers, we have been extravagantly forgiven of our darkest sins. On the cross, Jesus took each of them on himself, sacrificed his life, and paid the price for our disobedience.

Frail creatures that we are, we forget his mercy toward us so often. We get our feelings hurt or feel betrayed and entitled to anger. We then replay the offense and build a case against the person in our head. And in the end, *we* are the person who is harmed the most.

Resolve to not take God's grace for granted. If we daily confess our sins to God and then forgive others of sins they've committed against us, we will live in true freedom—just as he intended. Jesus taught his disciples to forgive others; we should follow his lead.

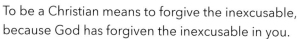

To be a Christian means to forgive the inexcusable, because God has forgiven the inexcusable in you.

C. S. Lewis

Forgiveness is setting the prisoner free, only to find out that the prisoner was me.

Corrie ten Boom

Forgiveness does not come easily to us, especially when someone we have trusted betrays our trust. And yet if we do not learn to forgive, we will discover that we can never really rebuild trust.

Billy Graham

For Further Reflection

Isaiah 43:25; Micah 7:18;
Matthew 6:12; 18:21-22; Luke 6:37

Today's Prayer

Lord, I want to live in freedom. Forgive me for nursing grudges and replaying offenses. Thank you for forgiving me so extravagantly of my sins! Help me to forgive others when they sin against me.
Amen.

Trusting Again

Some trust in chariots and some in horses, but we
trust in the name of the LORD our God.

PSALM 20:7

When you've been hurt, it's easy to build walls around your heart. You resist trusting others (especially anyone new) to prevent yourself from suffering more wounds. However, the same walls that help you feel safe also keep people out.

All of us need time to pull back after we've been hurt, but extended isolation is not God's desire for his children. He created us to find abundant life within the context of relationships. All of us need the affection and attention that healthy relationships provide. And while unsafe people do exist, we can't let that fact shut us off from laughter, love, and companionship.

But how do you trust again? Ask the Lord for courage to begin again; then ask a fellow Christian—a counselor, pastor, or friend—to pray for you to open your heart. Start slowly by giving or accepting an invitation to coffee or lunch. Rely on the Holy Spirit to give you discernment about which people to trust. Be patient with yourself and others, because everyone will fail you at some point . . . just as you will fail others. Finally, know that above all, you can rest in God's ultimate, perfect trustworthiness.

Our life is full of brokenness—broken relationships, broken promises, broken expectations. How can we live with that brokenness without becoming bitter and resentful except by returning again and again to God's faithful presence in our lives?

HENRI NOUWEN

Jesus often calls us to risk. He asks us to be vulnerable, to be authentic, so others can see Him in and through us.

MARY E. DEMUTH

Ask God to show you any changes you need to make in your relationships. And make sure your closest relationship continues to be with Jesus Himself.

DAVID JEREMIAH

FOR FURTHER REFLECTION

Deuteronomy 31:6; 2 Samuel 7:28;
Psalms 13:5; 28:7; 1 Corinthians 1:9

Today's Prayer

Faithful Father, I let hurts pile up and then I shut myself off from others. Give me the courage to have an open heart. Grant me discernment to find safe people in whom to trust. Amen.

Find Prayer Partners

*They all joined together constantly in prayer, along
with the women and Mary the mother of Jesus,
and with his brothers.*

Acts 1:14

In Matthew 18:20, Jesus said, "Where two or three gather in my name, there am I with them." Of course, he is with each one of us individually. But there is something inherently powerful when several people join in prayer.

How do you find people you can pray with? First, pray about it! God wants all of us to have friends and loved ones with whom we can share our requests and concerns. Maybe two or three of your close friends would welcome a regular prayer time.

Second, if you're not involved in a small group in your church, find one that is a good fit for you. (Just remember there are no perfect people, so there won't be a perfect group, either.) Listen to how they share, converse, and bear one another's burdens.

Third, ask friends and relatives how you can pray for them. They may be hesitant to share requests at first, so ask regularly. Don't force anything; just be kind and consistent. By creating a culture of prayer in your circle of influence, you will see lives change . . . including your own.

The spirit of prayer is more precious than treasures of gold and silver. Pray often, for prayer is a shield to the soul, a sacrifice to God, and a scourge for Satan.

John Bunyan

Nothing tends more to cement the hearts of Christians than praying together. Never do they love one another so well as when they witness the outpouring of each other's hearts in prayer.

Charles G. Finney

Prayer is the portal that brings the power of heaven down to earth. It is kryptonite to the enemy and to all his ploys against you.

Priscilla Shirer

For Further Reflection

Acts 20:36; 2 Corinthians 1:9-11;
Philippians 1:19; Revelation 8:4

Today's Prayer

Jesus, I want my prayers to be as powerful as yours were. I long to have fellowship in prayer with others, like the early church did. Lead me to people who will pray with and for me. And please remind me to pray for those who need it. Amen.

Tears Can Be Holy

Jesus wept.

JOHN 11:35

Tears can be holy. Think of a wounded veteran crying during physical therapy as he regains the use of his limbs or a father crying as his new baby is put in his arms. Picture the tears of a wife confessing sin to her husband as she asks for forgiveness. Or read today's Scripture and visualize Jesus weeping over a friend whose life was tragically cut short.

The fact that Jesus wept should give us comfort. We often say "I'm sorry" when we cry in front of others, but tears are nothing to be ashamed of. In fact, they are gifts from God. They are a sign of intense joy, pain, or grief.

Tears can reveal the beginning of an illness we haven't mentally registered yet, warn us of a boundary line that someone has crossed, help us get in touch with deep emotions we weren't previously conscious of, or signal that a beautiful gift has crossed our path.

Pay attention the next time you are brought to tears. What are they telling you? You might just be in the middle of a holy moment.

The sweetest things in this world today have come to us through tears and pain.

J. R. MILLER

Every tear of sorrow sown by the righteous springs up a pearl.

MATTHEW HENRY

I will not say: do not weep; for not all tears are an evil.

J. R. R. TOLKIEN

Sometimes we need the salt of tears to remind us how to savor the sweetness of life.

LYSA TERKEURST

FOR FURTHER REFLECTION

Psalms 56:8; 126:5; Luke 7:37–38, 44–47;
2 Corinthians 2:4

Today's Prayer

God, thank you for the gift of tears. They cleanse my heart and help me pay attention to both the joys and sorrows of life. Amen.

Fix Your Eyes on Jesus

Let us run with perseverance the race marked out for
us, fixing our eyes on Jesus, the pioneer and perfecter
of faith. For the joy set before him he endured the
cross, scorning its shame, and sat down
at the right hand of the throne of God.

HEBREWS 12:1–2

To be resilient through the ups and downs of life, we must fix our eyes on Jesus. In today's Scripture, Jesus is called "the pioneer and perfecter of faith." He is not only the source of the faith we profess; he is also the perfect embodiment of it. Because he loves us, we love the beautiful, messy, and sinful people around us (including ourselves). Because he sacrificed himself, we crucify our flesh daily. Because he endured death on the cross for the joy awaiting him in heaven, we can endure suffering, sickness, and so much more for the same joy.

We are sometimes ashamed of our weaknesses and struggles. We shouldn't be! Jesus could have been ashamed that he died on a Roman torture device, but he knew God's purposes and redemptive plan were worth his sacrifice.

He sat down at the right hand of God, and he now lives to intercede for us. He brings our names and needs before the Father—isn't that amazing? Fixing our eyes on that truth, we can persevere with hope.

The small and even overpowering pains of our lives are intimately connected with the greater pains of Christ. Our daily sorrows are anchored in a greater sorrow and therefore a larger hope.

HENRI NOUWEN

We have to be braver than we think we can be, because God is constantly calling us to be more than we are.

MADELEINE L'ENGLE

The secret of endurance is to remember that your pain is temporary but your reward will be eternal.

RICK WARREN

FOR FURTHER REFLECTION

1 Corinthians 13:6-7; Colossians 3:2;
2 Thessalonians 3:5; James 1:4, 12

Today's Prayer

Christ, I praise you for coming to save me, persevering to the cross, and rising again. Thank you for interceding for me. Help me fix my eyes on you, so I can endure until my last breath. Amen.

Light for the Dark Places

When Jesus spoke again to the people, he said, "I am the light of the world. Whoever follows me will never walk in darkness, but will have the light of life."

JOHN 8:12

In the beginning of Genesis, God commanded: "Let there be light," and light came into being (Genesis 1:1). It's comforting to meditate on the fact that wherever God dwells, there is light. In today's verse, we see that Jesus called himself the light of the world. We have that light in us.

So often, though, we unwittingly partner with Satan, who majors in darkness and shadows. We allow him to plant dark thoughts and then we meditate on them. We allow the violence and evil available on various media to penetrate the sanctuary of our homes, hearts, and minds. We foster negative attitudes, gossip about coworkers, and wish our political and personal enemies harm.

A truly healthy person is one who is filled to the brim with the things of God. Take inventory of the things you allow in your life. Do they have more in common with darkness or with light?

God longs to fill you up to overflowing with goodness, peace, patience, kindness, gentleness, and joy. When you allow him to infect every part of you, you are then a contagious Christian. You can spread God's light into dark places. And oh, how the world needs the light we have!

Where do you want God to shine his light? Ask him to dispel the darkness . . . and be willing to take steps toward the light today.

Christ is the true light of the world; it is through him alone that true wisdom is imparted to the mind.

JONATHAN EDWARDS

All the darkness in the world cannot extinguish the light of a single candle.

ST. FRANCIS OF ASSISI

While there remains one dark soul without the light of God, I'll fight—I'll fight to the very end!

WILLIAM BOOTH

FOR FURTHER REFLECTION

Exodus 13:21; Matthew 5:14-16;
Philippians 2:14-16; 1 Peter 2:9; 1 John 1:5

Today's Prayer

God of light, invade every part of me. Drive out the darkness of sin. Fill me to overflowing with your good gifts, and help me be a light that shines on others' paths to you. Amen.

Living with Uncertainty

As you do not know the path of the wind, or how the body is formed in a mother's womb, so you cannot understand the work of God, the Maker of all things.

ECCLESIASTES 11:5

Most of us are not good with change or uncertainty. We spend time and energy looking for—or creating a sense of—security in our jobs, homes, relationships, and even our internet service.

We also want security when it comes to our health, but health is difficult to be sure of. We seldom know whether the doctor we're seeing is certain or simply giving his or her best guess of a diagnosis. Medicines work one way with one patient and a different way with another. And our emotional health is dependent on factors we can't always control, like hormones, age, and genetics.

We also can't be sure of how God will answer our prayers or when he will do so. We are drawn to his power and mystery yet yearn for a game plan, some sense of what he's up to and how long it will take. However, faith calls us to trust in God, whom we can't see with our eyes, believing that he has perfect plans and will work all things for the good of those of us who love him.

One thing we can be sure of is God's love for us, which he proved once and for all on the cross. When you feel unsure of your next step or uncertain of God's purposes, dwell on the truths of Scripture and steady your heart in his unfailing compassion and provision for you.

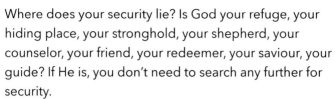

Where does your security lie? Is God your refuge, your hiding place, your stronghold, your shepherd, your counselor, your friend, your redeemer, your saviour, your guide? If He is, you don't need to search any further for security.

ELISABETH ELLIOT

Jesus Christ is not a security from storms. He is the perfect security in storms.

KATHY TROCCOLI

Christ can be trusted to keep His Word that He will exchange our drab existence for joyous living, abundant life! And while true love, total acceptance, and complete security are rare in our frantic world, the biblical evidence that our desires in these areas will be fulfilled in Christ is abundant.

JOSH MCDOWELL

FOR FURTHER REFLECTION

Job 42:2-3; Psalms 16:5; 18:32; 1 Peter 5:6-7

Today's Prayer

Lord, thank you for being unfailingly compassionate. I praise you for the ways you care for me, and I choose to rest in your sufficiency. You are my safe place, my security. Amen.

Jesus, Our Good Shepherd

*The LORD is my shepherd, I lack nothing. He makes
me lie down in green pastures, he leads me beside
quiet waters, he refreshes my soul.*

PSALM 23:1–2

Jesus is our Good Shepherd, the only way to eternal life. He sees to it that we are protected from the evil one who wants to destroy us, so we can pursue the peace only he gives. He leads us to quiet places when we need him to, refreshes our souls with his presence and his Word, and provides for our needs.

Isaiah 53:6 says "we all, like sheep, have gone astray." In the New Testament, Jesus tells us that he chases after even one lost sheep, like a shepherd who loves his flock and wants each one of them to be safe and whole (Matthew 18:12-14; Luke 15:4-7). In that parable, the shepherd also puts the lost sheep on his shoulders and carries it, illustrating the tender care he shows us when we are tired or hurt.

John 10:11-18 tells us that Jesus said he knows his sheep and his sheep know his voice. He also said that he would willingly give up his life for his sheep. On the cross, he did just that.

Thank Jesus today for all the ways he so lovingly shepherds you.

I am like the sick sheep that strays from the rest of the flock. Unless the Good Shepherd takes me on His shoulders and carries me back to His fold, my steps will falter, and in the very effort of rising, my feet will give way.

St. Jerome

God has not abandoned us any more than he abandoned Job. He never abandons anyone on whom he has set his love; nor does Christ, the good shepherd, ever lose track of his sheep.

J. I. Packer

It takes some of us a lifetime to learn that Christ, our Good Shepherd, knows exactly what He is doing with us. He understands us perfectly.

W. Phillip Keller

For Further Reflection

Isaiah 40:11; Ezekiel 34:12;
Matthew 9:36; Hebrews 13:20–21

Today's Prayer

Jesus, thank you for providing safety, food, shelter, and protection for me; and thank you for coming after me when I lose my way. Most of all, thank you for willingly giving up your life so I can be with you eternally. Amen.

A Quiet Heart

*I have calmed and quieted myself, I am like a weaned
child with its mother; like a weaned child
I am content.*

PSALM 131:2

These days, it's rare to find someone who displays a quiet heart. We're so used to being surrounded by people who are stressed out, busy, and distracted that when we find someone who seems settled, peaceful, and content, we're instantly drawn to him or her.

We can, however, cultivate quiet hearts for ourselves—growing contentment and peace—by soaking ourselves in God's Word and presence. The more we spend time with God, reading and meditating on his promises, the more our circumstances fade into the background.

When we settle our hearts in God, what we have and where we are satisfies us; and we don't feel like we need more to make us happy. We see how far God has brought us, not how far we think we have to go. Jesus becomes more real and present, and his supernatural peace calms our hearts. The Holy Spirit can then remind us of the verses we've learned—exactly when we need them.

If you already study the Scriptures, try listening to them as you drive or walk. Find scriptural songs to play as you do chores. Keep a Bible promise book with you to peruse while you're waiting for appointments, or download a Scripture app on your phone. See what a difference his Word can make.

If you look to others you will be distracted; if you look to yourselves you will be discouraged; but if you look to Christ you'll be delighted.

WARREN WIERSBE

A quiet heart is content with what God gives. It is enough. All is grace.

ELISABETH ELLIOT

If we are to say no to covetousness, we must learn to say yes to contentment. . . . Much of our discontentment may be traced to expectations that are essentially selfish and more often than not completely unrealistic.

ALISTAIR BEGG

FOR FURTHER REFLECTION

Psalm 119:49–50, 143–144, 165; Isaiah 32:17;
Philippians 4:11–12; 1 Timothy 6:6

Today's Prayer

Heavenly Father, I long for a quiet heart. Instead, I feel stressed and distracted. Help me find time each day to spend in your Word. Thank you for your precious promises, which calm my soul and bring me peace. Give me contentment and rest. Amen.

Ask for Wisdom

*Oh, the depth of the riches of the wisdom and
knowledge of God! How unsearchable his judgments,
and his paths beyond tracing out!*

ROMANS 11:33

G od told Solomon he would grant him anything
he wanted—and Solomon asked for wisdom.
Think of it: wisdom is such a valuable gift
that Solomon asked for it over power, honor, or wealth.
(Spoiler alert: God gave him all of those other things,
because he was pleased with Solomon's request
[1 Kings 3:1-15].)

Wisdom is invaluable for us if we're to truly lead a healthy
life. We need wisdom about what choices to make and
when to say no or yes. We need wisdom about which faith
community to take part in, what activities to join, and
what doctors or counselors to see. We also need wisdom
in our relationships with family members, coworkers, and
friends. Most of all, we need wisdom to be good stewards
of our time, energy, and resources.

In what areas do you especially need wisdom right now?
Take those concerns to God. He has unfathomable depths
of insight and knowledge . . . and he's waiting for you to
ask so that he can give those riches to you.

God's wisdom makes the glory of God's grace our supreme treasure. But man's wisdom delights in seeing himself as resourceful, self-sufficient, self-determining, and not utterly dependent on God's free grace.

JOHN PIPER

Prayer enables you to tap into God's wisdom anywhere, anytime, no matter what's going on.

ELIZABETH GEORGE

When the peace of God follows the purity of God's wisdom into our hearts and lives, it will affect those around us.

DAVID JEREMIAH

FOR FURTHER REFLECTION

Proverbs 2:6; 24:3; Isaiah 33:6; James 1:5; 3:17–18

Today's Prayer

God, I praise you for your unfathomable depths of insight and knowledge. Impart your wisdom to me when and where I need it most. Amen.

Walk with the Wise

Walk with the wise and become wise,
for a companion of fools suffers harm.

PROVERBS 13:20

As today's verse states, one way to get and keep wisdom is to walk with those who already have it. This Scripture doesn't mean that we should not have friends who are nonbelievers. God wants us to be friends with those who don't know him; how else will we share his love with those who need it? Rather, our wise Father knows that the people we are close to have a direct effect on our behavior.

In fact, according to an article posted at the Mayo Clinic website, the best kinds of friends can:

- Increase your sense of belonging and purpose
- Boost your happiness and reduce your stress
- Improve your self-confidence and self-worth
- Help you cope with traumas, such as divorce, serious illness, job loss, or the death of a loved one
- Encourage you to change or avoid unhealthy lifestyle habits, such as excessive drinking or lack of exercise
- Play a significant role in promoting your overall health

Pray for—and seek out—the right kind of friends for yourself. Our Father knows what you need, and he will guide you as you seek relationships with wise, godly people.

Thankfully, God brought wise Christian friends alongside to help me discover life-transforming precepts in his Word.

JONI EARECKSON TADA

You can't live the Christian life without a band of Christian friends, without a family of believers in which you find a place.

TIM KELLER

The next best thing to being wise oneself is to live in a circle of those who are.

C. S. LEWIS

He that would be himself wise must walk with those that are so, must choose such for his intimate acquaintance, and converse with them accordingly; must ask and receive instruction from them, and keep up pious and profitable talk with them.

MATTHEW HENRY

FOR FURTHER REFLECTION

Proverbs 15:7; 27:17; Ecclesiastes 7:5;
Daniel 12:3; Hosea 14:9

Today's Prayer

Jesus, you are the best friend I could ever hope for. Guide me as I seek out godly friends who act like you. Amen.

DAY 53

God Sees

[Hagar] gave this name to the LORD who spoke to her:
"You are the God who sees me," for she said,
"I have now seen the One who sees me."

GENESIS 16:13

In the story of the Egyptian slave Hagar and her master, Abraham, and mistress, Sarah, Hagar went to the desert wilderness twice. The first time, she went because Sarah was mistreating her after she got pregnant with Abraham's baby (Genesis 16:5–16). The second time, Abraham sent Hagar and her son, Ishmael, away after Sarah overheard Ishmael mistreating Sarah and Abraham's son, Isaac (Genesis 21:9–21).

Both times, God intervened in Hagar's life. In the first instance, he told her (through an angel) to go back to Sarah and submit to her. But that's not all: he also promised her that he would make her son into a great nation, and he told Hagar that he heard her misery.

In *Wounded Women of the Bible: Finding Hope When Life Hurts*, coauthor Tina Samples wrote:

> Hagar, in the middle of the desert, had an epiphany. An overwhelming presence fell upon her, and for the first time in her life, she understood something—God sees. "You are the God who sees me [El Roi]," she said. "I have now seen the One who sees me."

Wow! Hagar was the only woman in Scripture to name God.

Whatever you're going through, God sees what's happening. He cares. He knows. As you ponder El Roi, remember a time you felt seen and heard by someone you love—and what it felt like. That's how God is—all of the time.

God sees us with the eyes of a Father. He sees our defects, errors, and blemishes. But he also sees our value.

MAX LUCADO

God sees with utter clarity who we are. . . . He also sees who we are intended to be, who we will one day become.

JOHN ORTBERG

God sees everything at once and knows what you are called to do. Our part is not to play God, but to trust God—to believe that our single, solitary life can make a difference.

ZIG ZIGLAR

FOR FURTHER REFLECTION

Psalm 33:13; Proverbs 15:3;
Matthew 6:17-18; Hebrews 4:13

Today's Prayer

El Roi, thank you for seeing me, knowing all about me, and loving me. I give you praise and glory. What a difference your presence and knowledge make to me! Amen.

God Hears

This is the confidence we have in approaching God:
that if we ask anything according to his will,
he hears us.

1 John 5:14

D
o you ever feel as if your prayers are hitting the ceiling? That heaven is ignoring your call? Take courage, friend. The Word of God repeatedly says that God hears us when we call to him.

In fact, Isaiah 30:19 says: "People of Zion, who live in Jerusalem, you will weep no more. How gracious he will be when you cry for help! As soon as he hears, he will answer you." We may not see the answer right away, and it may not be the answer we most desire, but we can be comforted by the fact that God does answer our cries.

Proverbs 15:29 says: "The Lord is far from the wicked, but he hears the prayer of the righteous." Never fear oversharing with our heavenly Father. We simply can't tire him out.

If your feelings are overriding your faith, pray for more faith. (We know that God never says no to that request!) Ask him to help you believe more certainly that he loves you and listens to you.

Our God listens to us. Our God is a living God. He's not a block of wood you made up that's not going to answer you.

Francis Chan

God speaks in the silence of the heart, and we listen. And then we speak to God from the fullness of our heart, and God listens. And this listening and this speaking is what prayer is meant to be.

Mother Teresa

Some who attempt prayer never have the sense of anyone listening on the other end. They blame themselves for doing it wrong. . . . Prayer requires the faith to believe that God listens.

Philip Yancey

For Further Reflection

Psalm 145:19; Jeremiah 29:12–13;
John 9:31; 1 Peter 3:12; 1 John 5:15

Today's Prayer

Creator of all, thank you for listening to my prayers and answering them. I believe—help my unbelief. Amen.

God Restores

*Though you have made me see troubles, many and
bitter, you will restore my life again; from the depths
of the earth you will again bring me up.*

PSALM 71:20

Even if you've never tuned into the show *Fixer Upper* on HGTV, you've most likely heard about it. In the show, Chip and Joanna Gaines of Waco, Texas, restore life to properties available for sale, renovating houses to suit a family's needs. The show is popular because of the duo's chemistry, the laid-back attitude they have, and, of course, their talents at renovating homes. People value this couple's perspective and charm.

Did you know our God values restoration so much that the Hebrew word translated "restore" is used over and over again in the Old Testament? It's true! God's first promise to restore his people is in Deuteronomy 30:3, and it's repeated until its last use in Zechariah 10:6.

In "He Restores My Soul," Wayne Jackson wrote:

> A generous application of God's Word to our lives each day would do wonders for "restoring" mental stability. . . .

> Christ has the remedy for all ills that are not physiological in nature, and even when the ailments are physical, he can motivate us to endure by means of the encouragement within his sacred Word.

So spend some quiet time with God every day, and listen for his voice. Heed whatever instruction God has for you. You will feel better for it.

When God forgives, He at once restores.

THEODORE EPP

No matter who or what we are, God restores us to right standing with Himself only by means of the death of Jesus Christ.

OSWALD CHAMBERS

Most laws condemn the soul and pronounce sentence. The result of the law of my God is perfect. It condemns but forgives. It restores—more than abundantly—what it takes away.

JIM ELLIOT

FOR FURTHER REFLECTION

1 Kings 13:6; Psalms 41:3; 51:12; 80:3; 1 Peter 5:10

Today's Prayer

Heavenly Father, thank you for restoring my soul when I surrendered my life to you. Even now, you are restoring me and renewing me to make me more like you. You are such a good, giving, and gracious Father to me. Amen.

God Redeems

Let the redeemed of the Lord tell their story—those
he redeemed from the hand of the foe.

PSALM 107:2

Some of us are old enough to remember S&H Green Stamps. Grocery stores and other businesses gave away these lick-and-stick stamps (along with free books to put them in) whenever purchases were made. The more goods you bought, the more stamps you received. Eventually, you could redeem, or trade in, your stamps for merchandise at a local Green Stamp Store or from a catalog.

You and I have been redeemed, and our worth far exceeds the costliest item in any store. That God loves us so much that he was willing to have Jesus die for our sins on the cross should never cease to amaze us (John 3:16). Yet we have heard the story so often, we have a tendency to become numb to its full power. We tend to forget the fact that Jesus sacrificed himself for us—he died to redeem our souls.

Think of ways to thank and praise God for your redemption today. And while you're at it, share your redemption story with someone who hasn't heard it before. They need spiritual healing, too.

Christians can trust God to redeem even the greatest of tragedies and the most desperate of situations.

FRANKLIN GRAHAM

You've never gone too far that God can't redeem you, restore you, forgive you, and give you a second chance.

LYSA TERKEURST

God has given no pledge which He will not redeem, and encouraged no hope which He will not fulfill.

C. H. SPURGEON

FOR FURTHER REFLECTION

Exodus 6:6; Job 19:25; Luke 1:68; Galatians 3:14

Today's Prayer

Father God, I will never stop praising you for redeeming my soul. Yet sometimes, I forget just how costly that redemption was. Forgive me for letting it become stale. Restore to me the wonder of the cross—and show me whom to share that wonder with today. Amen.

The Helmet of Salvation

*Take the helmet of salvation and the sword of
the Spirit, which is the word of God.*

Ephesians 6:17

As children of God who have been purified by Christ, we can now wear the armor of God, the same garments as our Lord (Isaiah 59:17). Wow! But what does spiritual armor mean in practical terms to a healthy, whole Christian life?

The uppermost piece of armor is the helmet of salvation: it helps to protect our minds from the enemy's tortuous lies, similar to the way a Roman soldier's helmet protected his head and neck from enemy weapons (and from falling debris). Because we believe Christ died for our sins and rose again, we are Christ's possession, and the helmet of salvation is ours forever. The devil has no claim over us or our minds. He may try to invade our thoughts, but we have Jesus' resurrection power over him. Thank God for this defensive weapon! Without it, we would be vulnerable mentally; and that could lead to physical, emotional, and relational instability.

The next time you hear Satan spout his nonsense, declare—out loud—that he has no authority over you and must leave in the name of, and because of the blood of, Jesus.

There is a spiritual war mode that we must appropriate. It is an aggressive stance that we take against evil.

FRANCIS FRANGIPANE

The victory is already ours, the battle is already won; we have more than conquered whatever this world will try to throw at us because we're God's children; we have his kingdom in our hearts, and he loves us dearly.

CHRISTINE CAINE

God doesn't need a lot to do a lot. All David had was five stones. And all David used was one.

TONY EVANS

FOR FURTHER REFLECTION

Romans 13:12; 2 Corinthians 10:5;
Ephesians 5:11; 2 Thessalonians 3:3

Today's Prayer

Father, I bless your name. You have provided every weapon I need to withstand the devil's schemes. Thank you today for the helmet of salvation, which protects my thoughts. Amen.

The Shield of Faith

*Take up the shield of faith, with which you can
extinguish all the flaming arrows of the evil one.*

EPHESIANS 6:16

When Paul wrote about the shield of faith in his letters to the church at Ephesus, his readers would have envisioned a Roman soldier's shield; after all, the empire's soldiers were ubiquitous in their daily lives. Roman soldiers had huge shields, each made of wood covered with cloth and leather, with a metal boss in the center.

What's so interesting about Paul's choice of word picture here—he uses the Greek equivalent for *door* (*thyreos*)—is that each Roman shield was as big as a door and could practically protect the entire body of the soldier holding it, but it was light enough to be held in one hand. When facing an enemy attack of flaming arrows, the soldiers could dunk their shields in water to prevent the darts of their enemies from igniting these defensive weapons. Without their shields, Roman soldiers were extremely vulnerable to attacks of various sorts.

Without our shields of faith, you and I are also extremely vulnerable to attacks from our enemy, Satan. Our faith, however, is our protection against Satan and anything that he might throw at us to try to make us doubt what we know to be true.

Have you renewed your shield of faith by spending time in God's presence today? If not, do so now.

Be alert to the spiritual warfare around you.

HENRY BLACKABY AND RICHARD BLACKABY

Make no mistake: Satan's specialty is psychological warfare. If he can turn us on God ("It's not fair!"), or turn us on others ("It's their fault!"), or turn us on ourselves ("I'm so stupid!"), we won't turn on him. If we keep fighting within ourselves and losing our own inner battles, we'll never have the strength to stand up and fight our true enemy.

BETH MOORE

There is something about human nature that just doesn't want to face the reality that we live in two worlds. We live in the physical, material world where we have jobs, read books, and go about our business. And we live in a spiritual world—and that is a world at war.

JOHN ELDREDGE

FOR FURTHER REFLECTION

Genesis 15:1; Psalm 3:3;
Proverbs 30:5; 1 Peter 5:8–9

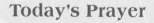

Today's Prayer

Lord, you are indeed my shield, protecting me from attacks by Satan. Forgive me for neglecting prayer and Bible study. I re-commit to a daily time of being in your presence, so I can continually renew my shield of faith. Amen.

The Sword of the Spirit

The word of God is alive and active. Sharper than any double-edged sword, it penetrates even to dividing soul and spirit, joints and marrow; it judges the thoughts and attitudes of the heart.

HEBREWS 4:12

God gave us several defensive weapons to use in spiritual warfare, but only one defensive weapon that also can be used as an offensive one. It is so powerful, though, that we need no other offensive weapon. This weapon is the Word of God, a sword that can be very effective in the hands of those who know how to use it, just like the Roman sword.

Usually between two and three feet long, the Roman sword, or *gladius*, which is surely what Paul wanted his readers to picture in their minds when considering the Word of God, was fearsome and mighty. The gladius was two-edged for cutting or slashing and was pointed so that it could be used for thrusting or stabbing. In skilled hands, it was a very valuable weapon, strong enough to pierce even metal armor.

When Satan or his demons attack, pull out the Word of God and do battle. The sword that the Lord gave you—the one he himself used against Satan in the wilderness (Matthew 4:1–11; Luke 4:1–13)—is all you need to defeat your enemy and continue your quest for wholeness.

Faith, prayer, and the Word of God are the weapons God provides you with to fight spiritual battles.

JIM GEORGE

If our children have the background of a godly, happy home and this unshakable faith that the Bible is indeed the Word of God, they will have a foundation that the forces of hell cannot shake.

RUTH BELL GRAHAM

Even on days when every cinder in our soul feels cold, if we crawl to the Word of God and cry out for ears to hear, the cold ashes will be lifted and the tiny spark of life will be fanned. For "the law of the LORD is perfect, reviving the soul."

JOHN PIPER

FOR FURTHER REFLECTION

Deuteronomy 33:29;
Psalms 17:13; 119:18, 160; James 1:21

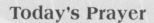

Today's Prayer

Heavenly Father, give me courage and discipline to study and apply your Word. Make me a warrior who fears nothing except losing touch with you. Amen.

The Belt of Truth

Stand firm then, with the belt of truth
buckled around your waist.

EPHESIANS 6:14

Not many of us think boldly and courageously when we hear the phrase "spiritual battle." Instead, we fret and worry that we won't be up to the challenge, or we think Satan knows us well enough that he'll find a chink in our armor. However, for our spiritual health to be strong, we need to stand up to our enemy. We can't do that alone—but we don't have to!

In today's verse, we are urged to stand strong with the belt of truth firmly in place. This belt is the truth found in the Word of God, which not only means the Bible but also the person of Jesus. In Paul's day, a Roman soldier's belt usually held a weapon or two and held his clothing tucked in place. But our belt holds the means to measure what the world has to say against what we know from Jesus and what the Bible says to be true. Without our belt of truth in place, we lose our singular focus on Jesus and his words of life, and the health of other areas in our lives—emotions, relationships, finances, work—tends to suffer.

God has a prescription to keep us in spiritual health: test everything against the truth of Scripture. Then you'll recognize the enemy's lies.

It is imperative that those who name the name of Christ
would be instructed in the truth of Scripture.

ALISTAIR BEGG

Instead of dissecting Scripture, we need to let Scripture
dissect us—our thoughts and attitudes, our dreams and
desires, our fears and hopes.

MARK BATTERSON

To trifle with Scripture is to deprive yourself of its aid.
Reverence it, and look up to God with devout gratitude
for having given it to you.

C. H. SPURGEON

FOR FURTHER REFLECTION

John 17:15-17; Acts 17:11;
1 Thessalonians 2:13; 5:20-21

Today's Prayer

Dear God, help me to test against the truth of your
Word everything I hear from the world. And help
me to keep my focus on you, Jesus, the living water
I can't live without. Amen.

The Breastplate of Righteousness

*He put on righteousness as his breastplate, and
the helmet of salvation on his head; he put on the
garments of vengeance and wrapped himself
in zeal as in a cloak.*

ISAIAH 59:17

Although Paul gives a complete description of
the armor of God in Ephesians 6:10-17, the
breastplate and helmet are first mentioned by
Isaiah (today's verse) and are described as being armor
that God puts on. The breastplate, or body armor, that a
Roman soldier put on was usually made of metal and was
his chief protection for the front and back of his body.
God's breastplate, and ours, is righteousness.

In the *MacArthur Study Bible,* pastor and scholar
John MacArthur described why the breastplate of
righteousness is our chief protection against our enemy:

> Because righteousness, or holiness, is such a distinctive
> characteristic of God Himself, it is not hard to
> understand why that is the Christian's chief protection
> against Satan and his schemes. As believers faithfully live
> in obedience to and communion with Jesus Christ, His
> own righteousness produces in them the practical, daily
> righteousness that becomes their spiritual breastplate.

Ask yourself: "Do I look like Jesus to other people?" Pray
that the Holy Spirit will reveal areas you need to work on,
and rely on his help to make necessary changes in your life.

Faith is the means by which the righteousness of Christ is given to us.

R. C. SPROUL

We shall never be clothed with the righteousness of Christ except we first know assuredly that we have no righteousness of our own.

JOHN CALVIN

For God does not want to save us by our own but by an extraneous righteousness which does not originate in ourselves but comes to us from beyond ourselves, which does not arise on our earth but comes from heaven.

MARTIN LUTHER

FOR FURTHER REFLECTION

Psalm 1:1-2; Micah 6:8; John 15:1-4;
2 Corinthians 7:1; James 2:21-24

Today's Prayer

Jesus, thank you for your righteousness. Because of your death and resurrection, I received it as a gift. What grace! Reveal areas that I need to work on to make me more like you. I will submit to your pruning, in faith that you have me in the palm of your hand. Amen.

Shoes Fitted with the Gospel of Peace

Stand firm then . . . with your feet fitted with the readiness that comes from the gospel of peace.

EPHESIANS 6:14–15

When we are fully resting in the righteousness of Christ, we will have a peace the world won't understand. However, the world will be drawn to it. And just as a Roman soldier's hard, studded shoes helped to keep his feet firmly on the ground, the gospel provides a firm foundation on which to base our lives.

A few years ago, gospel singer Steven Curtis Chapman's family endured a horrific loss when one of the older children accidentally ran over a younger child with his vehicle, killing her instantly. A few weeks after the tragedy, they appeared on *Larry King Live*. The television host, who is an avowed atheist, was noticeably bewildered—and moved—by the family's deep sense of peace during such a devastating event.

You and I have access to that same sense of peace. No matter what ups and downs life throws at us, we can find solace in our faith as we continue to read and study the gospel and apply it to our lives. We need to surrender our wills to God and cede control of our lives to him. When we truly give him the reins of our lives, no matter what happens, we will have his peace at the core of our lives. If you haven't felt that recently, voice a prayer of surrender and take a solid stand on the gospel.

Christ alone can bring lasting peace–peace with God, peace among men and nations, and peace within our hearts.

Billy Graham

Nothing will convince and convict those around us like the peaceful and positive way you and I respond to our hurts and distress.

Joni Eareckson Tada

Jesus made it possible for us to have the peace that passes all understanding–the kind that carries us, stabilizes us, grounds us, and keeps us from slipping.

Stormie Omartian

For Further Reflection

Isaiah 26:3; 32:17; John 14:27;
Romans 8:6; Philippians 4:7

Today's Prayer

Lord, the world desperately needs your peace, and so do I. Thank you for being the Prince of Peace in my life. Help me to stand firmly on your promises to me in the gospel. Amen.

Pray in the Spirit

Pray in the Spirit on all occasions with all kinds of prayers and requests. With this in mind, be alert and always keep on praying for all the Lord's people.

EPHESIANS 6:18

Paul finished up his advice on spiritual armor by reminding the church at Ephesus to be alert, pray in the Spirit on every occasion, and intercede for all of God's children. For Paul, prayer was as important a weapon as any other. He knew that concentrated prayer always leads to greater spiritual and emotional health, and it often precedes a change in our physical health, as well.

Paul also urged believers to pray "all kinds of prayers." God has given us a model of many kinds of prayer in his Word (the psalms alone include supplication, confession, praise, and intercession). And Jesus modeled prayer for his disciples by giving them what is now known as the Lord's Prayer: we are to praise God for his majesty, ask him for his will to be done and for our daily needs to be provided, ask for forgiveness for our sins as we forgive others' sins against us, and ask for protection from evil and temptation (Matthew 6:9-13).

Jesus and Paul both lived in a constant state of communion with God the Father. Humble, specific prayers were the key to their power and ministries—and you and I have access to that same divine, all-knowing power. As you go about your day, draw near to the Father in prayer—in full confidence that he hears you and is working on your behalf.

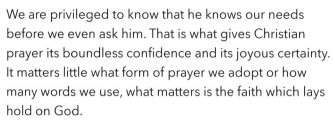

We are privileged to know that he knows our needs before we even ask him. That is what gives Christian prayer its boundless confidence and its joyous certainty. It matters little what form of prayer we adopt or how many words we use, what matters is the faith which lays hold on God.

DIETRICH BONHOEFFER

Prayer and praise are the oars by which a man may row his boat into the deep waters of the knowledge of Christ.

C. H. SPURGEON

Every great movement of God can be traced to a kneeling figure.

D. L. MOODY

FOR FURTHER REFLECTION

Psalms 6:9; 42:8; Matthew 6:5–8;
Romans 12:12; James 5:16

Today's Prayer

Jesus, I draw near to you in prayer. Thank you for giving me access to God the Father through prayer, and thank you for your example of how and when to pray. Increase my knowledge of you, and increase the health of every area of my life. Amen.

Our Strong Tower

Inside the city, however, was a strong tower, to which all the men and women—all the people of the city— had fled. They had locked themselves in and climbed up on the tower roof.

JUDGES 9:51

In biblical times, towers were used for several purposes, mostly to fortify and defend cities. Judges 9 describes how the Israelites who lived in Thebez climbed to "a strong tower" (verse 50) to defend themselves from Abimelek, an evil man who had murdered seventy of his brothers (verse 5) in order to become king and then sought to kill everyone who would not bow to his authority. (Fortunately, before Abimelek could light a fire to kill all the people in the tower, a woman dealt him a fatal blow by dropping a millstone on his head [verse 53].)

You and I have a strong tower in the person and name of our Lord. We also have a cornerstone—Christ—by which Satan's head was crushed (Genesis 3:15). The devil simply has no authority over us, and when he attacks, we can run to Jesus.

Is Satan trying to discourage and defeat you with insults, condemnation, or guilt? Use your weapons. Run to the arms of our Savior, and find a hiding place. Take strength from the fact that although Satan now roams this earth, killing and destroying, just like Abimelek, his eternal fate is sealed.

God is a place of safety you can run to, but it helps if you are running to Him on a daily basis so that you are in familiar territory.

STORMIE OMARTIAN

God will never let you sink under your circumstances. He always provides a safety net and His love always encircles.

BARBARA JOHNSON

If we belong to Christ, Satan has no right to exercise authority over us, but he hopes we're too ignorant regarding Scripture to know it.

BETH MOORE

FOR FURTHER REFLECTION

2 Samuel 22:2-3; Psalms 37:39; 61:3;
Proverbs 18:10; Nahum 1:7

Today's Prayer

Father, when I feel afraid, I will run to you. You are my strong tower, my place of refuge and safety. You make me brave enough to face my enemy. Amen.

When the Healing Won't Come

He said to her, "Daughter, your faith has healed you. Go in peace."

LUKE 8:48

In his Gospel, Luke described a woman who had spent twelve years going to doctor after doctor, trying to find a cure for her bleeding problem . . . all to no avail. But when she heard of Jesus' power, she knew she had to get close to him. In the middle of a large crowd, she reached to touch the hem of his garment—and was immediately healed. She didn't want to be noticed, but Jesus said, "Who touched me? . . . I know that power has gone out from me" (Luke 8:45-46). She came and fell at his feet, and Jesus told her, "Daughter, your faith has healed you."

This woman was healed, so why doesn't faith in Jesus heal everyone? The *NIV Quest Study Bible* explains it this way:

> God sometimes has a greater purpose than physical healing to accomplish in our lives: building character (Ro 5:3-4), teaching us to depend on him (2Co 12:7-10), allowing us to share in Jesus' suffering (1Pe 4:12-13), encouraging others toward faith through our example (Jas 5:10-11), and so forth. Faith, of course, is the ultimate healing; it brings eternal life in Jesus and the glorified bodies that believers will receive at the resurrection (1Co 15:50-57).

If God does bring miraculous healing, glorify him and testify about him. If he does not, pray for faith to glorify and testify about him just the same.

On a small scale, person-to-person, Jesus encountered the kinds of suffering common to all of us. And how did he respond? Avoiding philosophical theories and theological lessons, he reached out with healing and compassion.

PHILIP YANCEY

Healing comes when our story is raw, bone-deep and full of hunger for what only Jesus can offer.

DAN B. ALLENDER

God may remove your suffering, and that will be great cause for praise. But if not, He will use it; He will use anything and everything that stands in the way of His fellowship with you. So let God mold you and make you, transform you from glory to glory. That's the deeper healing.

JONI EARECKSON TADA

FOR FURTHER REFLECTION

Job 5:17–18; Isaiah 55:8–9; Jeremiah 17:14;
1 Peter 4:12–13, 19

Today's Prayer

Lord, forgive me for often wanting healing more than I want you, the Healer. Teach me how to trust in you, no matter how or when you answer my prayers. Amen.

A Thorn in the Flesh

*I was given a thorn in my flesh, a messenger of Satan,
to torment me. Three times I pleaded with the Lord to
take it away from me. But he said to me, "My grace
is sufficient for you, for my power is made perfect in
weakness." Therefore I will boast all the more gladly
about my weaknesses, so that Christ's power
may rest on me.*

2 CORINTHIANS 12:7–9

In Paul's second letter to the church at Corinth, he
revealed that in order to keep him from boasting, he
was given "a thorn in [his] flesh." He pleaded with
God to take it away, but God instead told Paul to rely on
God's power and grace to deal with the thorn.

Despite the fact that the thorn is never specified, the idea
of a "thorn" can be applied to our own lives. Perhaps
you have a physical condition or chronic illness. Maybe
you have a mental health challenge. Possibly you have
a recurring temptation that is hard for you to resist.
Whatever your specific "thorn," you can take comfort in
the fact that God is eternal, faithful, and never changing.
He is still strong in our weaknesses and has sufficient
grace to meet our every need.

God's power is often best displayed in the frail moments
of our humanity, and we can fall on Jesus when we are
tempted to despair or to wallow in self-pity. God made us,
so he knows us intimately. He also loves us perfectly. Can
you say with Paul, "I delight in weaknesses, in insults, in

hardships, in persecutions, in difficulties" (2 Corinthians 12:10)? If not, ask the Lord for help to see your trial as his opportunity.

I simply think God is greater than our weakness. In fact, I think it is our weakness that reveals how great God is.

MAX LUCADO

I discovered an astonishing truth: God is attracted to weakness. He can't resist those who humbly and honestly admit how desperately they need him.

JIM CYMBALA

All of us have areas of weakness. God wants these character flaws to teach us how totally dependent we are upon Him. When we handle them properly, they drive us into a deeper, more intimate relationship with the Lord.

CHARLES STANLEY

FOR FURTHER REFLECTION

Romans 8:26; 2 Corinthians 13:4;
Hebrews 4:15; 11:32–34

Today's Prayer

Abba Father, you know my every weakness. Be my strength and help me today and every day. Amen.

The Lord Is Our Banner

Moses built an altar and called it
The LORD is my Banner.

EXODUS 17:15

While the Israelites were at Rephidim, the Amalekites attacked them (Exodus 17:8-16). Moses told Joshua to pick men to battle their enemy, and then Moses himself climbed to the top of a hill with God's staff in his hands. Whenever he raised his hands with the staff, the Israelites began winning. However, when he lowered his hands, the Israelites began to experience defeat. Finally, Aaron and Hur decided to hold up Moses' hands when he got tired. The Israelites won, and there Moses built an altar, naming it "The LORD is my Banner" (*Jehovah Nissi* in Hebrew).

A banner is usually a flag or standard that represents a country, a cause, an organization, or a school that we are loyal to, a source of our inspiration and motivation. As our banner, God represents all that he is: love, protection, power, grace—so many wonderful things.

When we acknowledge that God is the source of everything that we have and we stay focused on him—when we make God our banner—the battle belongs to God. And we will find true, complete healing when we daily (or hourly, if necessary) lift our hands and hearts to him, saying "I belong to you."

Now is the time to know that God is able. To connect your current reality with God's present ability.

PRISCILLA SHIRER

Nothing is impossible for the people of God who trust in the power of God to accomplish the will of God.

DAVID PLATT

When you walk with Jesus, defeat turns into victory.

BETH MOORE

FOR FURTHER REFLECTION

Psalms 20:5; 60:4; 1 Corinthians 15:57; 1 John 5:4

Today's Prayer

Jehovah Nissi, I praise you for being my banner.
You give me the victory when I walk with you daily.
Thank you for being my source, guide, and goal.

Amen.

DAY 68

The Healing Power
of Gratitude

*Devote yourselves to prayer, being
watchful and thankful.*

COLOSSIANS 4:2

How often have you asked God for something in prayer and then forgotten to say "Thank you" after you've received an answer? Just like parents are pleased when their children express gratitude, God is pleased with our thankfulness. In fact, the Scriptures command us to be thankful.

It's no wonder God tells his people to express gratitude. After all, he created us, and he knows the healing power of thankfulness: it increases self-esteem and mental strength, helps people sleep better, encourages people to be more empathetic toward others, improves emotional and physical health, and promotes healthier relationships and appreciation of other people.

With those thoughts in mind, strive to add gratitude to your daily habits. For example, write five things you're thankful for in a journal before bed, or handwrite thank you notes (remember those?) for the next few gifts you receive. Make a list of verses that contain the word *thank* (or a variation of it), and meditate on them. Say "Thank you" to people you encounter often: a mail carrier or bank teller, a cashier or assistant. Better yet, thank your spouse and your best friend for always being there when you need them.

Thanksgiving is worry's kryptonite.

Matt Chandler

To be grateful is to recognize the love of God in everything He has given us—and He has given us everything.

Thomas Merton

When we were children we were grateful to those who filled our stockings at Christmas time. Why are we not grateful to God for filling our stockings with legs?

G. K. Chesterton

For Further Reflection

1 Chronicles 16:34; Ezra 3:11;
Psalms 107:21; 118:21; Hebrews 12:28

Today's Prayer

Lord, I long for a thankful heart. Create in me a spirit of gratitude, and remind me to share that spirit with others I encounter. Amen.

Resist Envy

A heart at peace gives life to the body,
but envy rots the bones.

PROVERBS 14:30

The advent of social media has given us many new catchphrases and acronyms. One new acronym is FOMO (fear of missing out). *Dictionary.com* defines FOMO as "a feeling of anxiety or insecurity over the possibility of missing out on something, as an event or an opportunity."

Of course, FOMO is nothing new. Social media has exacerbated the problem, though, because of the 24/7 availability of our accounts, as well as our ability to post on Instagram, Pinterest, Twitter, or Facebook only our best pictures from vacations and other moments we want to memorialize.

The problem is that other people also post their best moments, and we don't always remember that, so we end up comparing our worst moments—things we'd never post about—to other people's best. Then we become envious of their blessings, which is not good for us spiritually or physically. God wants us to be whole and holy, so he considers envy a sin.

If you struggle with envy, ask God to forgive you and help you see his gifts to you more clearly. Soon, you will feel joy at others' good fortunes, instead of being envious of them.

Envy is when you resent God's goodness in other people's lives and ignore God's goodness in your own life.

CRAIG GROESCHEL

The cure for the sin of envy and jealousy is to find our contentment in God.

JERRY BRIDGES

All the Christmas presents in the world are worth nothing without the presence of Christ.

DAVID JEREMIAH

FOR FURTHER REFLECTION

Exodus 20:17; Job 5:2; Mark 7:21-22; Galatians 5:26

Today's Prayer

Jesus, forgive me for envying others instead of rejoicing with them and for them. Give me strength to resist the temptation to be envious and resentful. Amen.

DAY 70

Persevere toward Healing

Not that I have already obtained all this, or have already arrived at my goal, but I press on to take hold of that for which Christ Jesus took hold of me.

PHILIPPIANS 3:12

Penny came from an emotionally abusive home. Not surprisingly, she married an emotionally abusive man, and together they had two children. Over time and with the help of her pastor and a codependency support group, she found the strength to erect healthy boundaries, which her husband continued to trample on. She separated from him and then he threatened her and the children with violence. Brokenhearted but resolved, Penny sought a lawyer and moved in with her parents. By then, she had a good relationship with her folks, who had owned up to their abusive behavior in the past.

Penny thought that getting away from her husband would make her life better, and it did . . . for a while. However, she began to experience bad dreams, anxiety attacks, and multiple health issues. Finally, she sought the help of a Christian twelve-step recovery program. She spent a year in the program and after completing it, she began to lead others through the steps.

It's been twelve years since Penny completed the program, and she acknowledges that she is still not fully healed. "But I'm getting there!" she says, with a big smile on her face. Where she once felt hopeless, she now feels joy.

Where she once felt useless, she now has purpose and plans. "I'm in process," she tells people. "But I'm loving life as I persevere toward my future."

Don't give in to despair if you're not where you want to be. None of us "arrive" fully until heaven. Keep persevering—and don't forget to enjoy the gifts God gives along the way.

By perseverance the snail reached the ark.

C. H. Spurgeon

Perseverance is more than endurance. It is endurance combined with absolute assurance and certainty that what we are looking for is going to happen. Perseverance means more than just hanging on, which may be only exposing our fear of letting go and falling. Perseverance is our supreme effort of refusing to believe that our hero is going to be conquered.

Oswald Chambers

For Further Reflection

Romans 5:3-4; James 1:2-4; 5:11; 2 Peter 1:5-6

Today's Prayer

Lord, how I need a spirit of perseverance! I get weary and discouraged. Renew my zeal for the path of healing I'm on. Thank you for how much you've already done in me; let me not falter on the road ahead. Amen.

DAY 71

Fuel for Healing

*Do you not know that your bodies are temples of the
Holy Spirit, who is in you, whom you have received
from God? You are not your own; you were bought at
a price. Therefore honor God with your bodies.*

1 Corinthians 6:19–20

God created our souls, minds, and bodies to
work together in harmony. When one is out of
balance, the other areas will also be off-kilter. So
what we put into our minds and our bodies matters.

Some Christians think that since we are not under the law
anymore, we can eat or drink or watch or read whatever
we want. "'I have the right to do anything,' you say—but
not everything is beneficial" (1 Corinthians 10:23). Think
about how you feel after eating a high-fat, high-sugar feast
versus how you feel when you eat healthy and drink lots of
water. There's a reason for that.

Starting today, note any ways you are not taking care of
your body. Maybe you don't get enough exercise; if so,
change your morning routine to include a couple of easy
exercises. (Don't forget to check with your doctor if you
haven't exercised in a while.) Maybe you eat too many
cookies or chips; if so, swap nutritious food for the junk
food. Each time you've formed a new habit, you've taken
another step toward good health. Your body—and soul—
will thank you for it!

God's Word is your owner's manual for life. It contains principles for health, finance, marriage, other relationships, business, and much more.

RICK WARREN

I resolved to dedicate all my life to God, all my thoughts, and words, and actions; being thoroughly convinced, there was no medium; but that every part of my life (not some only) must . . . be a sacrifice to God.

JOHN WESLEY

Whatever weakens your reason, impairs the tenderness of your conscience, obscures your sense of God, or takes off your relish for spiritual things . . . that thing is sin for you, however innocent it may be in itself.

SUSANNA WESLEY

FOR FURTHER REFLECTION

Proverbs 13:4; Daniel 1:11–16;
1 Corinthians 3:16–17; 10:31; 3 John 2

Today's Prayer

Father, I want to honor you in all I do, and I don't want to thwart your healing. Help me be a good steward of my body. Grant me self-control and strength to make healthy choices. Amen.

Don't Be Afraid to Say No

Am I now trying to win the approval of human beings,
or of God? Or am I trying to please people?
If I were still trying to please people,
I would not be a servant of Christ.

GALATIANS 1:10

If we can't say no, we'll run ourselves into the ground—or let others do it for us. Displaying Christian love doesn't mean submitting yourself to a life of busyness and striving. It doesn't mean pleasing people to the point of losing your core identity. What it does mean is that every decision is made with the wisdom of Christ, who dwells in us. If you've genuinely prayed and thought about something and believe that you shouldn't do it, you can say no without creating unnecessary angst for yourself.

If you've had problems saying no, start by asking yourself: "Why do I have a problem saying no? Am I afraid people will judge me? Do I care more about what people assume than what God thinks?" A tendency to say yes too much can be a sign of insecurity or finding your identity not in Christ but in others' expectations.

Believe it or not, "No" can be a complete sentence. If you truly feel that God has not called you to a task or activity, there is no need to defend yourself or make lists of reasons why you can't take it on. Instead, release yourself from the expectations of others, and move on.

If you desire to please God with the decision you make and afterward it proves to be a mistake, it's an error not an end.

Lysa TerKeurst

There is no work better than to please God; to pour water, to wash dishes, to be a cobbler, or an apostle, all are one; to wash dishes and to preach are all one, as touching the deed, to please God.

William Tyndale

Earthly wisdom is doing what comes naturally. Godly wisdom is doing what the Holy Spirit compels us to do.

Charles Stanley

For Further Reflection

Romans 12:2; Ephesians 5:8-10;
Colossians 1:9-10; 1 Thessalonians 4:1

Today's Prayer

God, I want to please you, not others. Give me wisdom and discernment as I strive to do so. Help me to say no (or yes) as you guide me. Amen.

Cast Away

For the sake of his great name the LORD
will not reject his people.

1 SAMUEL 12:22

In the movie *Cast Away*, a man survives a plane crash but is marooned on a deserted island for several years. He learns to survive by making fire and tools, eating fish, and working diligently on a boat made of parts of the washed-up airplane.

Sometimes, we can feel cast away by God. When our prayers are not answered in the way or time we expect, we begin to wonder if he is angry with us or is not listening at all. Doubts and fears assail us, and our faith falters.

We can take comfort in these times of darkness—when we can't see what God is up to or even feel his presence—by understanding that it happens to everyone. The biographies of heroes of the faith and biblical characters like Elijah and Job teach us that the important thing is to put one foot in front of the other and keep going. Eventually, the darkness will turn to light. God will rescue us, not because of what we have done, but because of his great compassion.

The Bible teaches again and again that God is ever-present, ever-loving, and ever-faithful. Hold on to that truth when *you* feel cast away.

I will have nothing to do with a God who cares only occasionally. I need a God who is with us always, everywhere, in the deepest depths as well as the highest heights. It is when things go wrong, when good things do not happen, when our prayers seem to have been lost, that God is most present.

MADELEINE L'ENGLE

If you are seeking to obey the Lord, expect opposition. Expect obstacles. Expect difficulties. But also expect God to see you through.

GREG LAURIE

As I am humbled by my difficulties, so I am strengthened by God's grace.

ALISTAIR BEGG

FOR FURTHER REFLECTION:

Deuteronomy 7:9; 31:8;
Psalms 18:16-19; 86:5; Hebrews 13:5

Today's Prayer

God, help me trust in your goodness and love for me, even when I can't feel or see you at work in my life. Amen.

An Unhurried Life

Show me, LORD, my life's end and the number of my days; let me know how fleeting my life is.

PSALM 39:4

One of the things God may need to heal is our schedules. In our culture, busyness is associated with productivity and status. So we pile activity upon activity, until our calendars are crammed fuller than a belly after Thanksgiving dinner.

All this rushing around leads to stress, health problems, and families who barely see one another. If you've eaten in your car more than three times this month, you might have fallen prey to busyness.

What would happen if more Christians decided to not play along with the frantic pace of this world? We would find our lives becoming healthier—and settled. People would notice that we were more rested, peaceful, and focused. They might wonder why and ask us about the difference in us.

Try pruning your schedule a bit over the next few weeks. Create margin for yourself and your family, and see how much better you feel—and how others react.

The busyness of things obscures our concentration on God. . . . Never let a hurried lifestyle disturb the relationship of abiding in Him.

OSWALD CHAMBERS

Ruthlessly eliminate hurry from your life.

DALLAS WILLARD

Are you in a hurry, flurried, distressed? Look up! See the Man in the Glory! Let the face of Jesus shine upon you—the face of the Lord Jesus Christ.

HUDSON TAYLOR

FOR FURTHER REFLECTION

Psalm 46:10; Jeremiah 2:25;
Mark 6:31; Luke 10:38-42

Today's Prayer

Jesus, you never hurried. Help me follow your example, because I know that my life is too busy. Show me how to take the time to live now—to get to know you better, to enjoy your blessings, and to spend more time with those closest to me. Amen.

Jesus, Our Deliverer

The LORD is my rock, my fortress and my deliverer;
my God is my rock, in whom I take refuge, my shield
and the horn of my salvation, my stronghold.

PSALM 18:2

Jesus, through his atonement for us, became our deliverer. As God used Moses to deliver the children of Israel from their oppressor, a wicked pharaoh who imposed slavery on them, Jesus freed us from our oppressor, Satan.

Because we've been delivered from an eternity separated from God, we no longer need to fear death. We can live with joy, even when suffering trials of all kinds, because of Christ's example and his indwelling power. We have the Word made flesh (John 1:1) and the Word of Scripture to guide and sustain us.

Such truths may have become old hat to you, if you've been a Christian for a long time; but old or new to Christianity, meditate on them once more. Praise God for his unconditional, sacrificial love, for righteousness we have not earned, and for our transformation. Praise him for healing you from the inside out. Praise him for delivering you from sin, sickness of soul, and living a purposeless existence. Finally, praise him for bringing you to—and through—the challenges that have made you who you are in him.

Never forget that God is far more interested in our getting to know the Deliverer than simply being delivered.

Beth Moore

God's path always delivers what He promises.

Billy Graham

God deliver me from the dread asbestos of "other things." Saturate me with the oil of the Spirit that I may be aflame.

Jim Elliot

For Further Reflection

1 Samuel 2:1; Psalm 144:2; Daniel 3:17;
Romans 7:25; 2 Corinthians 1:10

Today's Prayer

Precious Lord, thank you! You were delivered over to sinful men so that you could deliver me. I praise you for being my rock, fortress, shield, and deliverer. Amen.

The Healing Power of Solitude

*After he had dismissed them, he went up on a
mountainside by himself to pray. Later that night,
he was there alone.*

MATTHEW 14:23

Whether you enjoy being alone or not, it's wise to make space in your schedule for solitude. Although you might feel energized by always being around people, a need to constantly be with other people might be a sign that some emotional wound needs healing—fear, PTSD, or simple insecurity. Even if that is not the case, a few quiet moments by yourself will allow you to feel energized in a much different way.

Spiritually, it's hard for God to whisper to us when we're surrounded by noise and people, so we're more likely to hear him when we're quiet and by ourselves. Our time alone with God can spiritually power us, enabling us to better cope with whatever the day brings our way. Our example for this is Jesus, who often withdrew to be alone and hear from his Father.

If you're not comfortable being alone, start with a short amount of time. Don't turn on the television or computer; just sit with your thoughts for a few moments. Make time to do this every day.

Above all, remember that in Christ, you are never truly alone . . . and you need not feel lonely.

It is in lonely solitude that God delivers His best thoughts, and the mind needs to be still and quiet to receive them.

CHARLES SWINDOLL

If you meet God in solitude, you discover the God you meet is the God who embraces all people.

HENRI NOUWEN

Spending some time getting quiet can really be the best remedy for tangled situations. Taking a step back from all the emotion, frustration, and exhaustion to sit quietly with Jesus will do more to untangle a mess than anything else I've ever found.

LYSA TERKEURST

FOR FURTHER REFLECTION
1 Kings 19:11-13; Habakkuk 2:20;
Matthew 6:6; Luke 5:16

Today's Prayer
Father, I want to hear from you. Forgive me for too often surrounding myself with noise and people instead of withdrawing to a quiet place to be alone with you. Slow me down and settle my heart, so I can listen to what you have to say to me. Amen.

The Hope of Glory

God has chosen to make known among the Gentiles
the glorious riches of this mystery, which is
Christ in you, the hope of glory.

Colossians 1:27

We hope for healing, for fulfilled dreams, and for heaven. But one thing we could never imagine on our own, which is almost beyond comprehension, is the fact that God now lives in us and through us because of Jesus.

Not only that, but Jesus continues to heal and transform us more and more into his likeness the longer we serve him (2 Corinthians 3:18). And our hope of heaven is secure because he substituted his life for ours on Calvary. Now, if that doesn't make you want to dance and shout, check your pulse!

As we find ourselves healed of sins, sickness, and wrong thinking, we are compelled to share his hope with others. Then we become what Henri Nouwen called "wounded healers." We remember our scars—and accept them—because God has overcome them and is using them for his glory. And when others get hope from us, they begin to share it in their circles, and that leads to changed lives and the angels celebrating around the throne.

Pray that God would allow you to share your ongoing story of healing and hope with someone new. Then be watchful for the opportunity to do just that.

The Christmas message is that there is hope for a ruined humanity—hope of pardon, hope of peace with God, hope of glory—because at the Father's will Jesus Christ became poor and was born in a stable so that thirty years later He might hang on a cross.

J. I. PACKER

Hope is called the anchor of the soul (Hebrews 6:19), because it gives stability to the Christian life. But hope is not simply a "wish" (I wish that such-and-such would take place); rather, it is that which latches on to the certainty of the promises of the future that God has made.

R. C. SPROUL

FOR FURTHER REFLECTION

Job 11:18; Psalms 25:5; 42:5;
Romans 5:1-2; Hebrews 6:19-20

Today's Prayer

Savior, you alone—not fame or fortune, success or status—are my hope of glory. Thank you for continuing to heal me. Give me opportunities to share my story—and yours—with those who need hope. Amen.

God, Our Father

Our Father in heaven, hallowed be your name.

MATTHEW 6:9

Those of us who have or had fraught relationships with our earthly fathers find it difficult to square God's character as a perfect father with our own experiences. How do we overcome such dysfunction?

By studying the attributes and character of God and drawing close to him in faith, we begin to see him for who he is and stop equating him with our earthly fathers. As we dwell in God's presence and Word, and experience fulfillment of our deepest longings for peace and home, we can replace the picture of God we had with the truth of who he really is.

If you have a hard time with God as Father, speak to your pastor or a Christian counselor about it. Express yourself honestly to God in prayer. (After all, if God weren't okay with questions, Job would have been wiped off the earth!) Finally, lean into God by faith. Your feelings will begin to follow as the Holy Spirit works in you.

Rest in this fact: Jesus called his Father "Abba," which most closely resembles our word *daddy* (Mark 14:36). Children often call their father "Daddy" when he is good, kind, and compassionate. And that describes your heavenly Father exactly.

This is and has been the Father's work from the beginning—to bring us into the home of his heart.

GEORGE MACDONALD

Snuggle in God's arms. When you are hurting, when you feel lonely, left out, rejected, let Him cradle you, comfort you, reassure you of His all-sufficient power and love.

KAY ARTHUR

The heavenly Father will not break his word to his own child.

C. H. SPURGEON

The life of faith is a daily exploration of the constant and countless ways in which God's grace and love are experienced.

EUGENE PETERSON

FOR FURTHER REFLECTION

Psalm 68:5; Isaiah 9:6; John 1:12; 16:27;
Romans 8:14

Today's Prayer

Lord, in my humanness, I get confused about who you are. Thank you for being compassionate, kind, and good. I will claim that truth and rest in it, today and every day. Amen.

No Room for Condemnation

There is now no condemnation
for those who are in Christ Jesus.

Romans 8:1

D o you live under a gray cloud of guilt?
Condemnation is one of Satan's fondest tools
for limiting our effectiveness as believers. He
knows he cannot separate us from God eternally, but he
will create false guilt in us by bringing up our past sins.
Then we have a tendency to wallow in the mud and muck
of condemnation, instead of rebuking Satan and claiming
the truth of the gospel.

Friend, condemnation is not of God. Yes, he convicts
us—to bring us to repentance. However, our salvation was
purchased by the blood spilled on the cross of Christ.
Therefore, we don't have to live under a cloud of shame
or guilt.

If you've never received the gift of salvation, don't delay
any longer. Surrender your past, present, and future to
the loving, nail-scarred hands of Jesus. If you have, and
you are still struggling with condemnation, do a Scripture
study on God's forgiveness. Then live in the healing,
freeing truth you find—one step at a time.

The Law was given by Moses; the moral law, to discover
the extent and abounding sin; the ceremonial law, to

point out, by typical sacrifices and ablutions, the way in which forgiveness was to be sought and obtained. But grace, to relieve us from the condemnation of the one, and truth answerable to the types and shadows of the other, came by Jesus Christ.

JOHN NEWTON

If you look at your past and are depressed it means that you are listening to the devil.

D. MARTYN LLOYD-JONES

Your past, present, and future are taken care of as you put your trust in Jesus.

RICK WARREN

FOR FURTHER REFLECTION

Psalm 31:1; Romans 5:16–18;
2 Corinthians 3:9; Ephesians 1:7

Today's Prayer

Righteous One, I thank you that I don't have to live under a cloud of regret, shame, and guilt. I put my trust in you and praise you for your forgiveness. Help me to embrace my standing as righteous before you because of the cross. Amen.

DAY 80

The Importance of Accountability

Jonathan said to David, "Go in peace, for we have sworn friendship with each other in the name of the LORD, saying, 'The LORD is witness between you and me, and between your descendants and my descendants forever.'"

1 SAMUEL 20:42

Jonathan and David shared a bond, a commitment, to each other that was reflected in their loyalty to each other and a lasting trust between the two. They could share with and encourage each other. An accountability partner or group can do the same for us. By sharing our goals, progress, and setbacks with others, we can find support and strength.

It's fairly well known that when someone has an accountability partner, the chances of that person achieving his or her goal is greatly increased. In other words, when you have to report your progress (or lack of it) to someone, you actually have a much better chance of success. Accountability is key to success.

Pray about asking a friend to join you in your quest for better physical or spiritual health and wholeness. You can share goals together weekly or monthly. It may just speed up your progress—and you'll deepen a friendship.

If you could benefit from a group, seek out a twelve-step or support group.

The road to spiritual and physical health is less lonely—
and often shorter—when we find an accountability partner
or group. So don't delay.

Everyone says they want community and friendship. But
mention accountability or commitment to people, and
they run the other way.

Tim Keller

We do not find the meaning of life by ourselves alone—
we find it with another.

Thomas Merton

Is any pleasure on Earth as great as a circle of Christian
friends by a good fire?

C. S. Lewis

For Further Reflection

Proverbs 12:26; 27:17; Ecclesiastes 4:9–12;
Galatians 6:1–3; 1 Thessalonians 5:11

Today's Prayer

Lord, lead me to people in whom I can confide and
with whom I can find accountability. Amen.

When Healing Becomes an Idol

Do not turn to idols or make metal gods for yourselves. I am the LORD your God.

LEVITICUS 19:4

During times we desperately desire to be healed, we can place too much importance on a future day when God answers our prayers the way we expect. We then bargain with God, telling him that if he'll only heal us completely, we will serve him / surrender to his leading / stop a certain behavior forever.

One of the problems with this kind of thinking is that it treats God's blessings as a transaction instead of undeserved favor (grace). It's as if we see God as a vending machine who dispenses answers to prayer when we've met some requirement he has set. This cheapens grace and elevates our healing to the status of an idol—something we worship instead of God alone.

Search your heart and ask the Father if you have made healing an idol in your life. If you have, repent and ask his forgiveness. Begin to thank God for all he's already done, and as you continue to pray for more healing and transformation, ask the Holy Spirit to convict you if you put that idol back on the throne—where only God belongs.

Every one of us is, even from his mother's womb, a master craftsman of idols.

JOHN CALVIN

A god who let us prove his existence would be an idol.

DIETRICH BONHOEFFER

An idol of the mind is as offensive to God as an idol of the hand.

A. W. TOZER

FOR FURTHER REFLECTION

Exodus 34:17; 1 Samuel 12:21;
Psalms 31:6; 106:36; Jonah 2:8

Today's Prayer

Father, I confess I have made an idol out of my healing. Forgive me. I want to worship you and you alone. Thank you for the many ways you have already blessed me. Amen.

The Duality of Emotions

Trust in the LORD with all your heart and lean not on your own understanding.

PROVERBS 3:5

Emotions are God-given, and we cannot deny their power. In fact, emotions can be indicators, and we should be in touch with our emotions enough to find out the *why* behind whatever we're feeling. For instance, if we feel upset every time we're around a certain person, we should review our interactions with them to find clues as to why we feel that way. Once we understand what's behind our feelings, we can make changes.

However, we cannot live solely by our emotions. As Elisabeth Elliot wisely said in her book *Quest for Love: True Stories of Passion and Purity*:

> The difficulty is to keep a tight rein on [our] emotions. They may remain, but it is not they who are to rule the action. They have no authority. A life lived in God is not lived on the plane of the feelings, but of the will. In Scripture the heart *is* the will—it is the man himself, the spring of all action, the ruling power bestowed on him by his Creator, capable of choosing and acting.

As you go through your day, notice your emotions, but don't let them overtake what you know to be God's will for you. Use the sword of the spirit—and the rest of your spiritual armor—to fight against the ways Satan would use your feelings to prevent you from being obedient and victorious in faith.

We shall never find happiness by looking at our prayers, our doings, or our feelings; it is what Jesus is, not what we are, that gives rest to the soul.

C. H. Spurgeon

Sight is not faith, and hearing is not faith, neither is feeling faith. . . . Therefore we must believe before we feel, and often against our feelings, if we would honor God by our faith.

Hannah Whitall Smith

[God's] love is not a passing fancy or superficial emotion; it is a profound and unshakable commitment that seeks what is best for us.

Billy Graham

For Further Reflection

Proverbs 4:23; 16:32; 28:26;
Jeremiah 17:9; 1 John 3:20

Today's Prayer

God, thank you for giving me emotions. They make me human! Help me to discern when my feelings are leading me astray, and give me strength to withstand the enemy's schemes. Amen.

Jesus Frees Us

It is for freedom that Christ has set us free.
Stand firm, then, and do not let yourselves
be burdened again by a yoke of slavery.

GALATIANS 5:1

C hrist is a liberator. Some he sets free from slavery to fear, helping them walk free. Some he sets free from busyness, reorganizing their time to make God and family a priority. And he liberates all who believe from death and eternal separation from God.

It seems counterintuitive to our materialistic, me-first culture that surrendering your life, time, and possessions would lead to joy and fulfillment, but it's true: the most joyous people in the world are those who follow Jesus, without fear, into whatever he's called them to do.

What is Jesus calling you toward? Whether he has set you free from debt, disease, or doubt, he wants you to help others find freedom. Pray about the ways he may want you to follow him. As he leads, tell and show other people the ways and methods by which he has healed you.

People who think they are free eventually end up slaves to their own desires, and those who give their freedom away to the only One you can trust with that freedom eventually get it back.

PHILIP YANCEY

Truth is more important, freedom is more complex, and Jesus is more liberating than you think.

Tim Keller

When you believe God is who he says he is, when you hang onto him and his Word in faith, his truth sets you free.

Christine Caine

For Further Reflection

Psalm 119:145; Isaiah 61:1;
2 Corinthians 3:17; Galatians 5:13–14

Today's Prayer

Jesus, you have been so good to me. Show me when and how to share about the freedom and healing you have given me. Amen.

DAY 84

Learning to Reframe Our Lives

Since, then, you have been raised with Christ, set your hearts on things above, where Christ is, seated at the right hand of God. Set your minds on things above, not on earthly things.

COLOSSIANS 3:1–2

Have you ever heard the term *reframing*? It means looking at something from a different perspective, and it's a very powerful concept to learn and utilize. Let me give you an example.

In *When Changing Nothing Changes Everything: The Power of Reframing Your Life,* author Laurie Polich Short writes about an attractive married man she met at a Christian conference. She was single, and they had an undeniable connection, but she chose not to follow her feelings because she knew that the fallout would be too great. Later, she heard that the man had had an affair; and she knew that he hadn't wanted her—he'd wanted out of his marriage. Short wrote,

> The ability to reframe and view yourself in the middle of your story enables you to rest in *what is,* knowing that it is part of what is taking you to *what will be.* Things are happening in you—and to you—and if you attempt to escape your circumstances, rather than live them, you may actually abort a process that could be bringing something wonderful into your life.

Think of the places in your life where you feel in the

middle. Take strength and patience from the Lord as you live those circumstances fully, not wishing you were somewhere else (or with someone else). Trust the process, because it is governed by a loving Father.

I must learn that the purpose of my life belongs to God, not me. God is using me from His great personal perspective, and all He asks of me is that I trust Him. . . . When I stop telling God what I want, He can freely work His will in me without any hindrance.

OSWALD CHAMBERS

The essence of wisdom, from a practical standpoint, is pausing long enough to look at our lives—invitations, opportunities, relationships—from God's perspective. And then acting on it.

CHARLES STANLEY

FOR FURTHER REFLECTION

Genesis 50:18-20; Esther 4:14;
Psalm 139:23-24; Philippians 4:8, 12

Today's Prayer

Father, teach me to see my circumstances from an eternal perspective. Help me make decisions with the end—not the middle—in mind. Amen.

God Can Use Anything

Isaiah said, "Prepare a poultice of figs." They did so and applied it to [Hezekiah's] boil, and he recovered.

2 Kings 20:7

You may have heard people say that we should have enough faith for God to heal us without medicine (especially if you've suffered from depression or anxiety). However, that belief is not based in biblical truth. Of course, we need to be responsible and prudent when we take medications, and we need to be under a doctor's care. But medicines are quite miraculous in themselves!

In Scripture, God healed people using various methods. He had Elisha tell Naaman to wash seven times in a river (2 Kings 5:1-19), and he had another prophet apply a healing poultice (today's verse). Jesus healed with a word (John 4:49-50), a touch (Luke 4:40), the hem of his garment (Matthew 9:20-22), and even dirt covered with spit and washed off (John 9:6-7).

And today, like then, God uses many different methods to heal his children. He created science and plants, so he can (and does) use medicines. He uses counselors, support groups, and pastors to help us heal emotionally and spiritually—if we partner with them and do the work they ask us to. God can use exercise to further heal us after surgery, but we must be willing to put in the time doing physical and/or occupational therapy.

Be open to the different methods God can use to heal you.

If Jesus heals instantly, praise Him. If Jesus heals gradually, trust Him. When Jesus heals ultimately, you will understand.

MAX LUCADO

Jesus reveals a God who does not demand but who gives; who does not oppress but who raises up; who does not wound but who heals; who does not condemn but forgives.

BRENNAN MANNING

You see, you are a spirit, you have a soul, and you live in a body. You have emotions, you have thoughts, you have a will, and you have a conscience. You are a complex being! And Jesus came to heal every single part of you. There's not one part that He doesn't want to make completely whole.

JOYCE MEYER

FOR FURTHER REFLECTION

Ezekiel 47:12; Mark 6:13;
Acts 19:11-12; 28:8-9; James 5:13-14

Today's Prayer

God, you continue to heal people in many different ways. Help me to be open to your various methods and to do my part when necessary. Amen.

What Lazarus Can Teach Us

The sisters sent word to Jesus, "Lord, the one you love is sick."

JOHN 11:3

Mary and Martha were grief-stricken. Their brother, Lazarus, had been very ill, and they sent word to their close friend, Jesus, asking him to come to their side in Bethany. Jesus got their message but stayed where he was. He only appeared in Bethany after Lazarus had died and been in the grave for several days.

Jesus didn't tarry out of unconcern or cruelty. Instead, he knew God's plan for Lazarus, and he wanted to show Martha, Mary, and their brother a new level of healing. Jesus came—too late, they thought—and wept, embracing his friends in empathy and compassion; and then he called Lazarus out of the grave, and the dead man obeyed. The sisters, along with everyone who stood beside them in their time of suffering, got their brother back . . . and Jesus got his friend back.

Think about the things you longed for God to do—now or in the past. Maybe God is tarrying out of love, not callousness. Perhaps he wants to resurrect, or bring forth again, something that has been dead to you or in you, and maybe that can only occur if he allows you to wait or to suffer. If you need faith to trust him, ask him for it. And reread the story of Mary, Martha, and Lazarus (John 11:1–44).

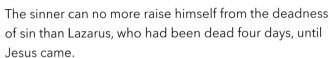

The sinner can no more raise himself from the deadness of sin than Lazarus, who had been dead four days, until Jesus came.

GEORGE WHITEFIELD

The possibility of transformation is the essence of hope.

JOHN ORTBERG

Pain and trials are almost constant companions, but never enemies. They drive me into His sovereign arms. There He takes my disappointments and works everything together for good.

KAY ARTHUR

FOR FURTHER REFLECTION

Job 33:4; Isaiah 42:5–7; Luke 16:22–25;
John 5:21; 2 Corinthians 3:18

Today's Prayer

Holy God, you are the giver of life and breath. Give me greater faith. Bring forth in me everything you desire. Resurrect anything dead in me, that I may give more glory to you. Amen.

Conflict as an Opportunity

Blessed are the peacemakers,
for they will be called children of God.

MATTHEW 5:9

Conflict is an opportunity to grow in the grace and knowledge of Christ, to demonstrate his peace in the midst of disagreement and division, and to reflect the identity we have as children of God. Our world is full of conflict, but we can show non-Christians a gospel-oriented way to solve it—if we're willing to.

Most of us, however, don't run toward conflict; in fact, we often run away from it. As Christians, though, we are in a unique position to try to create an atmosphere, a culture, of harmony and peace. To do so requires wisdom and discernment, patience and practice—but it is possible.

Ask yourself: "How do I see conflict? Do I usually run away from it? Why (or why not)?" Then pray for an open heart and mind to see conflict in a new way: as an opportunity to share the grace you have received from God and to demonstrate God's grace to others.

God actually rises up storms of conflict in relationships at times in order to accomplish that deeper work in our character.

A. W. Tozer

Conflicts bring experience, and experience brings that growth in grace which is not to be attained by any other means!

C. H. Spurgeon

Lord, help us to accept the pains and conflicts that come to us each day as opportunities to grow as people and become more like you.

Mother Teresa

For Further Reflection

Jeremiah 1:7-8; Matthew 18:15-17;
Romans 12:17-19; James 3:18; 1 Peter 3:15

Today's Prayer

Father, I want to see conflict as an opportunity and not a threat. Show me how to change my perspective. Then please help me to be a peacemaker. Amen.

Pursue Peace

Make every effort to live in peace with everyone and
to be holy; without holiness no one will see the Lord.

HEBREWS 12:14

Pursuing peace in the midst of conflict is difficult, but not impossible, especially once you realize that we are all different by God's design, but are also all created in God's image. In other words, just because we're different or want different things doesn't mean we can't get along together.

An introvert—someone who prefers to be left alone—might have a conflict with an extrovert—someone who prefers to spend more time together. Neither person is wrong; they're just different. So compromise is the key to finding peace. Unfortunately, when one of the people decides that his or her needs are more important than the other's needs, their desires become an idol, and peace becomes hard to come by. Both people end up missing out on God's best and on being able to do what God wants in and through them.

The point is that when conflict arises, the pathway to peace is treating each other in a Christlike manner, seeking to serve the other person, and glorifying God in the process.

Think about your desires. Which desires have led to the most conflict, and why? Pray for wisdom to see the difference between healthy desires and idolatrous ones, and ask God to heal you of selfishness, self-deceit, and idol making.

Let nothing disturb you, / Let nothing frighten you, / Though all things pass / God does not change.

St. Teresa of Ávila

We think that idols are bad things, but that is almost never the case. The greater the good, the more likely we are to expect that it can satisfy our deepest needs and hopes. Anything can serve as a counterfeit god, especially the very best things in life.

Tim Keller

Whatever we trust in or love is an idol if it replaces the true God. . . . Idolatry is about me—my desires, my wants. My purpose is not to exalt the idol above myself, but to use the idol to give me what I want.

Edward T. Welch

For Further Reflection

John 13:34–35; Romans 14:13; 15:7;
Colossians 3:13; James 4:1–3

Today's Prayer

Jesus, you are the Prince of Peace. Give me a Christlike spirit, so I can pursue peace with others. Forgive me when I've let my desires become demands and when I have set up idols.

Amen.

God's Economy

Praise be to the God and Father of our Lord Jesus
Christ, the Father of compassion and the God of all
comfort, who comforts us in all our troubles, so that
we can comfort those in any trouble with the comfort
we ourselves receive from God.

2 CORINTHIANS 1:3–4

O nce God has comforted us in our troubles, we can then comfort those around us with the same love and compassion God has for us. God's economy often works this way: What we may see as weakness, God chooses to make strong—and he gets the glory. What we may see as a negative, God turns into a positive—and he gets the glory.

Think of the story of Joseph: Joseph was hated and sold into slavery by his brothers. Later, he was promoted to Potiphar's assistant, but Potiphar's wife had him thrown in prison after he rebuffed her advances. He languished for two years before he interpreted Pharaoh's dreams and became Pharaoh's right-hand man. He eventually met his brothers again and forgave them. Because of his position, Joseph was used by God to save the children of Israel from starvation during a terrible famine (Genesis 37, 39–47).

Joseph knew what we can sometimes only grasp in hindsight: what Satan means to use for evil, God can use for good. What part of your story could you use to encourage others? In what ways has the Lord comforted you—and with whom can you share that comfort?

Suffering is seldom an item on our list of requests to the Lord. But when it crosses our path and we are able by His grace to keep on walking, our lives become messages of hope to the world and to the church.

SHEILA WALSH

Vision is the ability to see God's presence, to perceive God's power, to focus on God's plan in spite of the obstacles.

CHARLES SWINDOLL

Tonight, no matter what you're going through . . . backtrack and remember all the places where God has been so faithful before in your life. And know. Know with assurance. And boldness. And confidence. He is the same faithful God.

LYSA TERKEURST

FOR FURTHER REFLECTION

Psalm 86:17; Isaiah 49:13; Romans 12:13, 15;
1 Thessalonians 2:7–8

Today's Prayer

Almighty God, thank you for the ways you turn things around. Use my experiences and trials for your glory, and show me how to give comfort to others who have been through things I've been through. Amen.

God Fights for Us

*Moses answered the people, "Do not be afraid. Stand firm and you will see the deliverance the L*ORD *will bring you today. The Egyptians you see today you will never see again. The L*ORD *will fight for you; you need only to be still."*

EXODUS 14:13–14

Shortly after Moses started to lead the chosen people out of Egypt, the people became desperately afraid because the Red Sea was on one side of them and Pharaoh's pursuing army was on the other. In their humanness, they couldn't see a way out of the situation. They wanted to give up and give in.

But God is a master at turning desperate circumstances into displays of his glory. Exodus 14 describes how God made a way through the Red Sea for his chosen people. Then, after Pharaoh's armies started to follow the people onto the riverbed, God caused the waters to collapse on top of them.

God will do the same for us when our backs are up against the wall. We don't have to be afraid. We can be still, knowing he fights for us. Sometimes, it takes dire straits for us to see straight into his heart and find out exactly who he is.

This is how God works. He puts people in positions where they are desperate for his power, and then he shows his provision in ways that display his greatness.

DAVID PLATT

Desperation compels us to pray with fervent, focused faith—especially when we have no one else to turn to. God honors our faith when we place it in him alone—with no back-up plan, no other recourse, no other way out. He hears and answers our desperate heart cry, because he loves to show himself strong on our behalf.

ANNE GRAHAM LOTZ

God has a plan for our deliverance before our problems ever appear. He is not surprised when trouble comes. He is not in Heaven wringing His hands trying to figure out what to do. He's in control. Our part is to focus on Him and His mighty power, worshipping Him and praising Him for the manifestation of His solution and listening for a word of direction from Him.

JOYCE MEYER

FOR FURTHER REFLECTION

Deuteronomy 20:4; Joshua 1:5; Psalm 34:17;
Isaiah 41:11-13; Romans 8:31

Today's Prayer

Lord, sometimes I see no way out of my circumstances. Give me faith to trust that you will never let me down. Thank you for your power and your promise to fight on my behalf. Amen.

Rest in God

Truly my soul finds rest in God;
my salvation comes from him.

PSALM 62:1

S ome days, we're just flat-out tired—bone-deep, soul-weary tired. On those days, we may not feel we have the strength to do our part in order to heal: exercise, eat well, think right, be with people, go to church, meet with our accountability partner or our support group, or visit a doctor. We may not even have the energy to read the Bible or pray. Instead, we want to stay in bed and pull the covers over our heads.

It's okay to withdraw from the world—for a short period. Everyone needs a break now and then. Just don't run from God and the world for more than a few hours. God wants us to participate in life, not be spectators.

Know this: when you feel like you can't move another step, God is patient and gentle. You don't need to hide your weariness from the Father. He knows you so well, he already knows what you're thinking and feeling. You can—and should—bring all of yourself to God—not just the shined-up parts. When all you feel is weary, you can rest, knowing that he is ever-constant and never tired. And he never stops working on your behalf.

In place of our exhaustion and spiritual fatigue, God will give us rest.

Charles Swindoll

Rest time is not waste time. It is economy to gather fresh strength. . . . It is wisdom to take occasional furlough. In the long run, we shall do more by sometimes doing less.

C. H. Spurgeon

Once I knew what it was to rest upon the rock of God's promises, and it was indeed a precious resting place, but now I rest in His grace. He is teaching me that the bosom of His love is a far sweeter resting-place than even the rock of His promises.

Hannah Whitall Smith

For Further Reflection

Exodus 20:8–11; Psalms 3:5; 105:4;
Isaiah 30:15; Matthew 11:28–30

Today's Prayer

Father, you know how weak and weary I am. Help me rest in you, knowing you are never tired. Thank you that you never cease working and moving on my behalf. Amen.

God's Healing in Relationships

Above all, love each other deeply, because
love covers over a multitude of sins.

1 PETER 4:8

God desires to heal our relationships with friends and loved ones. Although some relationships will never be fully healed this side of heaven, we can do a few things to start the healing process here and now. First, we can own up to our own sins and wrong choices. A good apology says, "I was wrong, I hurt you, and I'm sorry." (Don't make excuses or say "If I hurt you . . ." or "I'm sorry you got your feelings hurt.")

Second, if another person has hurt or harmed us in some way, we can offer forgiveness to them, even if they don't repent. Third, we can be steadfast and strong, not allowing ourselves to get sucked into too much drama. We can set healthy boundaries while still serving and loving the other person. Fourth, we can—and should— put distance between us and the other person if the relationship becomes manipulative or toxic in any way.

Finally, we can pray for God's healing power to work on us and the other person. God is in the miracle business, after all, and one of the chief ways he shows his power is through life-change.

People are unrealistic, illogical, and self-centered. Love them anyway.

MOTHER TERESA

Christianity is not a religion or a philosophy, but a relationship and a lifestyle. The core of that lifestyle is thinking of others, as Jesus did, instead of ourselves.

RICK WARREN

If I'm not showing grace . . . have I forgotten the grace I've been shown?

JOHN MACARTHUR

FOR FURTHER REFLECTION

Leviticus 19:18; Proverbs 28:13;
Matthew 6:14–15; Galatians 5:22–23

Today's Prayer

Lord, heal my broken relationships. And let the healing begin with me. Amen.

DAY 93

Healing Speech

May these words of my mouth and this meditation
of my heart be pleasing in your sight, Lord,
my Rock and my Redeemer.

PSALM 19:14

Every day, we say thousands of words. How many of them display the fruit of the Spirit (Galatians 5:22–23)? How many are kind, good, and gentle? How many of them are loving, patient, and peaceful? How many of them reflect joy, faithfulness, and self-control? Maybe we tend to gossip around the water cooler at work, so we can feel like part of the group. Perhaps we lack self-control when we chat with our friends about our spouse, thinking it's okay to make fun of them and talk them down when we're with the gang.

We can't conjure up the spiritual fruits, of course, but as we spend time with God and his Word, growing in maturity, we should start to look more like Jesus. People who hear us talk and watch us interact with others should be able to tell that there is something different about us. Our words can be healing in a world full of hurt.

If using words wisely is an area you struggle with, first ask the Father to forgive careless words you've spoken. Second, consider whether you need to ask people you've talked about to forgive you. Finally, study Proverbs—the book is full of verses about using words both wisely and unwisely. It has thirty-one chapters, so you can carefully read a chapter a day over a month.

Perhaps we have been guilty of speaking against someone and have not realized how it may have hurt them. Then when someone speaks against us, we suddenly realize how deeply such words hurt, and we become sensitive to what we have done.

THEODORE EPP

If I speak what is false, I must answer for it; if truth, it will answer for me.

THOMAS FULLER

Words which do not give the light of Christ increase the darkness.

MOTHER TERESA

FOR FURTHER REFLECTION

Job 4:4; Psalm 141:3; Matthew 15:11;
Ephesians 4:29; 1 Peter 3:10

Today's Prayer

Lord, forgive me for so often speaking careless, unkind words. Grow in me the fruit of the Spirit, that I may be different from the world and bless others with the words I say. Amen.

Free Indeed

If the Son sets you free, you will be free indeed.

JOHN 8:36

Our Savior was taken prisoner, so we would be set free. He was sentenced to death, so we could find life. He was unjustly accused, so we can resist the devil. He was crucified, abandoned, and rejected, so we could have eternal life, fellowship with God, and acceptance.

That Jesus set us free is a fact. It's a reality. To live in that reality means to live in grateful awe and worshipful reverence and to make every decision in light of his atoning sacrifice. Since grace wasn't cheap for him, we shouldn't cheapen it by assuming that since we are saved, we can act how we want to.

How could you show your gratitude and awe to God today? Ask the Holy Spirit for ideas. Perhaps you could write a poem or song of worship, pen a letter of thanks, or tell someone in your life about how Jesus freed you. And as always, you can act out your faith and seek to be Christlike.

If our gospel does not free the individual up for a unique life of spiritual adventure in living with God daily, we simply have not entered fully into the good news that Jesus brought.

DALLAS WILLARD

When we become captive to the Word of God, then we discover true freedom.

ALISTAIR BEGG

Come, thou long expected Jesus, / born to set thy people free; / from our fears and sins release us, / let us find our rest in thee.

CHARLES WESLEY

FOR FURTHER REFLECTION

Psalm 119:45; Romans 6:22;
Philippians 2:5; 1 Peter 2:16

Today's Prayer

Jesus, I am unquestionably grateful to you for your death, resurrection, and ascension. Help me show my gratitude and awe in all I say and do. Amen.

All of God's Promises
Are Yes in Christ

*No matter how many promises God has made, they
are "Yes" in Christ. And so through him the "Amen"
is spoken by us to the glory of God.*

2 Corinthians 1:20

Did you know that once you believe in Jesus, once
you repent and accept God's forgiveness, God is
ever faithful to you? His promises are true. And
he blesses you with peace—and abundant life.

Maybe you've been beaten down by life, and people
have rarely kept their promises to you. If that has been
the case, it's natural that you would feel hesitant about
trusting others. However, once you've walked with God
for a time, when you think back over your relationship to
God and how he's worked in your life, you will start to see
patterns. His delays and denials make sense when you see
from his perspective. And those terrible circumstances
you were forced to endure? They were made bearable by
his grace, and you had his strength to compensate for
your weakness.

When the devil hits you with doubt, remind him of
today's Scripture. Every one of God's promises was
fulfilled—and will continue to be fulfilled—through
Jesus Christ.

My imperfections will never override God's promises. God's promises are not dependent on my ability to always choose well, but rather on His ability to use well.

LYSA TERKEURST

The stars may fall, but God's promises will stand and be fulfilled.

J. I. PACKER

One of the great enemies of hope is forgetting God's promises.

JOHN PIPER

FOR FURTHER REFLECTION

Joshua 23:14; Psalm 145:13; Romans 4:16-17;
2 Peter 1:3-4; 1 John 2:25

Today's Prayer

Heavenly Father, thank you for your very great and precious promises. I praise you that every promise is yes in Jesus. Amen.

Where, O Death,
Is Your Sting?

Where, O death, is your victory?
Where, O death, is your sting?

1 Corinthians 15:55

Our culture is death-obsessed. We fear the walking dead, but we make it a hit television show. We say we hate violence, but we spend millions of dollars on violent video games and horror/slasher movies. And we celebrate Halloween, a holiday dedicated to the macabre. Yet we almost never talk about death, even though every one of us will face it.

Because of the cross, we no longer need to fear death. We can look it in the face and say, "Where is your victory? Where is your sting?" Also, we don't have to fear that we will never see our believing loved ones again. Jesus set us free from that torment, as well. We know that we will be reunited in heaven with those we love, because he promised it would be so.

Praise God for this infinitely comforting fact and for his gift of eternal life through the cross.

I do not fear death. I may fear a little bit about the process, but not death itself, because I think the moment that my spirit leaves this body, I will be in the presence of the Lord.

Billy Graham

At the heart of Christian faith is the story of Jesus' death and resurrection.

JOHN ORTBERG

I don't so much pray that my death will be without pain, but that it will be without doubt.

JOHN PIPER

Death is no more than passing from one room into another. But there's a difference for me, you know. Because in that other room I shall be able to see.

HELEN KELLER

FOR FURTHER REFLECTION

John 11:25–26; 14:1–3; Romans 5:10;
1 Corinthians 15:21; 2 Timothy 1:9–10

Today's Prayer

Jesus, thank you that by your atoning sacrifice, you eradicated the need to fear death for all of us who believe. Amen.

Spiritual Gifts
and Healing

*There are different kinds of gifts, but the same Spirit
distributes them. There are different kinds of service,
but the same Lord. There are different kinds of
working, but in all of them and in everyone
it is the same God at work.*

1 CORINTHIANS 12:4–6

God created each of us a certain way for a reason. And each of us has been given at least one spiritual gift from God, a gift we are to use to build up the body of Christ. The spiritual gifts include everything from administration to wisdom, from evangelism to prophecy, from compassion to mercy—to name just some of the twenty or so gifts listed in the Bible (Romans 12:6-8; 1 Corinthians 12:8-10; 1 Peter 4:11). Any spiritual gift God has given you can be used to encourage others as they journey toward healing.

For example, someone with the gift of teaching could lead others in studies of Scriptures that discuss healing. A person with the gift of administration could plan an event showcasing groups or organizations that help people heal. Someone with the gift of servanthood could provide support in one form or another (a ride, the time to listen, a shoulder to lean on)—whatever will help someone heal.

Pray about your gift, and ask God for ideas on how to use your gift in service to him and to others—both to give him glory and help others heal.

Your spiritual gifts were not given for your own benefit but for the benefit of others, just as other people were given gifts for your benefit.

RICK WARREN

As God's children, we are not to be observers; we're to participate actively in the Lord's work. Spectators sit and watch, but we are called to use our spiritual gifts and serve continually.

CHARLES STANLEY

You have inside you the capacity to invest your mental, emotional, and spiritual gifts in a way that glorifies God, impacts the world, and satisfies your own soul. I believe that—and I want you to believe it, too.

DAVID JEREMIAH

FOR FURTHER REFLECTION

Romans 12:3-4; 1 Corinthians 14:12;
Ephesians 4:4-8, 15-16; 1 Peter 4:10

Today's Prayer

Father, thank you for my spiritual gift. Show me how to use it to show your love and to help others. Amen.

Does Time Heal All Wounds?

Now is your time of grief, but I will see you again and you will rejoice, and no one will take away your joy.

JOHN 16:22

Phrases like "Time heals all wounds" and "God helps those who help themselves" are often spouted in times of crisis. But they are not biblical, and they are more harmful than helpful.

God, not time, heals all wounds. And grief is a journey and a process, not a straight line from sad to happy. Also, no two people grieve in the same way. You may find yourself deeply sad years after a traumatic event (especially on certain days that hold significant meaning). That doesn't mean you haven't healed at all; it simply means you may still have areas of your heart that need special attention and care.

Be patient with yourself, just as God is patient with you. Try not to rush the healing process—in you or anyone else. Our Father alone knows what your process of healing will be. Trust him to complete it, as he wills. And know that although now might be your time of grief, you will one day be full of joy in God's presence because of Jesus.

For in grief nothing "stays put." One keeps on emerging from a phase, but it always recurs. Round and round. Everything repeats.

C. S. Lewis

Our griefs cannot mar the melody of our praise, we reckon them to be the bass part of our life's song, "He hath done great things for us, whereof we are glad."

C. H. Spurgeon

Real grief is not healed by time. . . . If time does anything, it deepens our grief.

Henri Nouwen

For Further Reflection

Psalm 10:14; Lamentations 3:32;
Matthew 5:4; Revelation 21:4

Today's Prayer

Father, I know that you are the true healer of every type of wound. Help me to trust that you know my pain and will give me the patience to let you heal me in your own timing. Amen.

God Will Complete What He Started

[Be] confident of this, that he who began a good work
in you will carry it on to completion
until the day of Christ Jesus.

PHILIPPIANS 1:6

G od promises that whatever work he has begun, he will complete. It may not be as quick as we would hope—in fact, it may take a lifetime—but he will not leave the tapestry of grace he's weaving unfinished. We can trust that he is working in and through us exactly how he planned.

Think about Moses. He started as a miracle baby snatched from the jaws of death by Pharaoh's daughter. He was a work in progress: after being raised in luxury, he killed an Egyptian and went into hiding; he questioned God, even when the Creator spoke out loud to him (through a burning bush, no less!); and he needed a spokesman in order to talk to Pharaoh. However, God used Moses to deal severely with the Egyptian taskmasters and to set the Israelites free from slavery. And Moses led the children of Israel faithfully through the desert wilderness.

Claim the promise from Philippians for yourself. In fact, write today's verse on a sticky note and place it on your computer, car dashboard, or bathroom mirror where you can see it often. God will, indeed, finish what he started—in you and in all of creation.

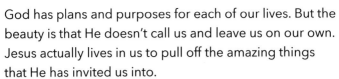

God has plans and purposes for each of our lives. But the beauty is that He doesn't call us and leave us on our own. Jesus actually lives in us to pull off the amazing things that He has invited us into.

LOUIE GIGLIO

When you yield yourself in complete and wholehearted obedience to God, He can do great things through you.

JIM GEORGE

Contentment is the equilibrium between the enjoyment of life now and the anticipation of what is to come.

PRISCILLA SHIRER

FOR FURTHER REFLECTION

Deuteronomy 32:4; Psalm 139:13–16;
Jeremiah 29:11; Colossians 2:10

Today's Prayer

Father God, complete the work you've begun in me. I thank you for the amazing promise that you will finish every good thing you've started in my life. Amen.

Finishing Well

I consider my life worth nothing to me; my only aim is to finish the race and complete the task the Lord Jesus has given me—the task of testifying to the good news of God's grace.

ACTS 20:24

After his dramatic conversion from approving of Stephen's stoning to being a believer in Jesus, Paul had one goal: to preach the salvation message to as many people as possible, for as long as possible, until the Lord took him to heaven.

That puts our paltry (though worthy) goals—lose weight, pay off our credit cards, spend more time with the kids—to shame, doesn't it? When we think about the future, we must hold it loosely. We don't know how long God will give us on earth; we should pray to be good stewards of the limited time we have.

Try not to get caught up in the temporary trappings of this world. Instead, fix your eyes on Jesus and focus on glorifying him with every thought, word, and action. Stay the course and complete the tasks he has set before you.

May each of us finish well.

My legacy doesn't matter. It isn't important that I be remembered. It's important that when I stand before the Lord, he says, "Well done, good and faithful servant." I want to finish strong.

JAMES DOBSON

Life is the only race you'll run where you don't know where the finish line is.

STEVE FARRAR

All things are possible to him who believes, that they are less difficult to him who hopes, they are more easy to him who loves, and still more easy to him who perseveres in the practice of these three virtues.

BROTHER LAWRENCE

FOR FURTHER REFLECTION

Psalm 63:1; 1 Corinthians 9:24;
Galatians 6:9; 2 Timothy 4:7; Hebrews 12:1

Today's Prayer

Jesus, help me finish well—as you did. Amen.

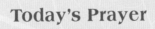

DEVOTIONALS FROM
STEPHEN ARTERBURN

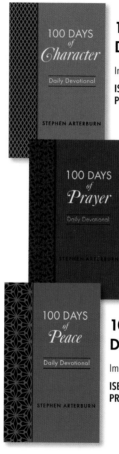

100 Days of Character
Daily Devotional

Imitation Leather, 208 pages, 5" x 8"

ISBN: 9781628624953
PRODUCT CODE: 4172X

100 Days of Prayer
Daily Devotional

Imitation Leather, 208 pages, 5" x 8"

ISBN: 9781628624281
PRODUCT CODE: 4138X

100 Days of Peace
Daily Devotional

Imitation Leather, 208 pages, 5" x 8"

ISBN: 9781628624960
PRODUCT CODE: 4173X

www.hendricksonrose.com